BOSH!
ON A BUDGET

NUMBER ONE BESTSELLING AUTHORS
HENRY FIRTH & IAN THEASBY

HQ
An imprint of HarperCollinsPublishers Ltd
1 London Bridge Street
London SE1 9GF

www.harpercollins.co.uk

HarperCollinsPublishers
1st Floor, Watermarque Building, Ringsend Road
Dublin 4, Ireland

10 9 8 7 6 5 4 3 2 1

First published in Great Britain by
HQ, an imprint of HarperCollinsPublishers Ltd 2021

ISBN: 978-0-00-842070-3

Exclusive Edition ISBN: 978-0-00-849823-8

This book is produced from independently certified FSC™ paper
to ensure responsible forest management.

For more information visit: ww.harpercollins.co.uk/green

Photography [food]: Lizzie Mayson
Photography [portrait]: Nicky Johnston
Food Styling: Rosie Ramsden
Prop Styling: Sarah Birks
Design and Art Direction: Studio Polka
Commissioning Editor: Zoë Berville
Project Editor: Dan Hurst
Cover Design: Stephanie Heathcote

Printed and bound in Italy by Rotolito.

CONTENTS

WELCOME!

Hi everyone, thanks for picking up this book!

As humans, we are great at looking at what's right in front of us, we're okay at remembering the past, but what we're not so good at is looking to the future. Perhaps that's why, despite all the apocalypse movies and scientists predicting it, we didn't spot the pandemic waiting for us. Maybe that's why we've messed up the climate, too.

What we, as a species, are really good at, is making the best out of what is put in front of us and working out how to survive in any situation. Even though it's been a tough few years, all things considered the human race has done pretty well!

We all stayed at home. Heroic key workers did their jobs in masks, while the rest of us said 'goodbye' to the daily commute and 'hello' to working from our sofas. We binge-watched TV while answering emails. Face-to-face meetings became video calls. Some got dressed up for the occasion and some did Zoom meetings in their pyjama bottoms. (You know who you are!)

And with our new-found homeyness, we fell back in love with cooking! Lunches became major occasions rather than momentary reprieves from office life. Dinners became date nights and major events.

We baked bread – banana, white, sourdough, lockdown loaves – until the flour ran out. We bought pasta, and lots of it, until the shelves ran dry. We made big batches of quick and cheap curry and chilli, knowing we'd be home to eat them! We paid more mind to breakfasts, preparing granola and oats to brighten up boring mornings. And when the supermarket shelves were bare, we cooked our way through our pantries. Dried lentils and chickpeas were picked off cupboard shelves for the first time in months to make delicious soups, curries and salads.

We also learned about the benefits of eating fruits and vegetables for our immunity. Doctors on TV talked about the benefits of garlic, ginger, turmeric and cinnamon. We learned how Vitamin D and washing our hands could help keep us healthy. We drank a few more green smoothies (even if we then ate lovely choccy bars to stave off the mid-afternoon boredom afterwards).

Social distancing kept us away from our fellow humans to stop viruses passing between us and growing even more mean. Hopefully, at least some of us spared a thought for the poor pangolin or bat – patient zero – and pondered whether we should all be eating more plants after all. Those poor creatures certainly weren't socially distanced!

And many of us tried to save money. Holidays were all but cancelled for 2020; even 'staycations' were only allowed for a brief precious time in the summer. For those working, routines became cheaper. For the many who lost their jobs or were helped out by the government, saving money became even more important. While it may have been driven by hard times, focusing on saving the pennies has been a great skill for us to learn. Saving money is an act of planning for your future. It's literally a gift for your future self. We can all do it. And thinking about the cost of what we put in our bodies is the best place to start.

As the crescendo of our love letter to you all, we'd like to celebrate the fact that, as luck would have it, the most affordable way to eat is also the best way! Eating plants is not only great for your pocket, it's also super healthy for your body and great for the planet too.

The fruit and veg that are the building blocks of vegan cuisine are just plain delicious, with the added bonus of being cheap too. Through this, perhaps our best book yet, we will show you how to take these building blocks and use them to create incredibly delicious, affordable, plant-based meals that will keep you coming back time and again.

We hope you love the recipes as much as we do.

Big love to you all, and Happy Cooking!

Henry and Ian

ABOUT THIS BOOK

How should you save money and cook good food? What does 'budget' actually mean? The answer is different for everybody. We thought about making you a price promise – 'every recipe under blah' – but we decided against it as the cost of a dish depends so much on where and how you shop. We settled on a budget meal typically costing about £1 to £2 per portion, and that's what you'll find in this book. Some may push that by a few pennies, but many, many more come in far below that. So, whatever budget means to you, we've got you covered.

Convenience costs money, so we've gone back to basics in this book in a way that we never have before. Making some staples yourself, instead of buying them, is a lovely way to spend your time and a cheaper way to cook, and it also gives you a better end product. In this book you'll find a chapter on Staples (pages 220–243) with recipes for basics such as Home-made Tofu (page 222), Stocks (page 234), Home-made Pasta (page 227) and a couple of home-made breads (pages 240 and 242). Cooking basics yourself is far more rewarding than buying stuff in. You don't have to make every loaf of bread yourself, but if you've got a bit of time on a weekend, give it a go. You'll have learnt a new skill, have something to be really proud of and save yourself a bit of cash in the process. Win, win, win!

To help you budget, we've thought of the seasons too. Flick through this book and you'll see recipes that change and adapt depending on the season. Seasonal fruit and veg tastes better, costs less and is better for the planet, so it was really important for us to include a seasonal aspect to these recipes. (You can read more about seasonal fruit and veg on pages 12–19).

Batching is a powerful skill to have in your arsenal – it will save you time and money too. In this book you'll find a batching element to many of the recipes, as it's such an efficiency hack. Batch recipes empower you to feed the freezer, so you've always got a healthy home-made meal ready to cook when you don't have time to cook from scratch. Who needs expensive takeaways anyway? (More on batching can be found on pages 28–29).

The most exciting thing about this book is that the recipes are not only budget friendly, they are also absolutely delicious and bursting with flavour. That's the BOSH! way! So you can expect the same big bangin' flavours and scrumptious results, just with a more careful eye on the bottom line. BOSH!

COOKING WITH THE SEASONS

It's easy to forget about seasonal food, as supermarkets have everything available all year round! But all that convenience comes at a price, and not just a financial one. Produce that is out of season is often shipped in from abroad (always check the label to see where your fruit and veg hails from!), racking up food miles and depleting in flavour as it makes its way to the supermarket shelves. It's also not great for the planet to be shipping stuff all the time. Fruit and veg that are in season are fresher, tastier, better for the planet and generally cheaper – it's a no-brainer! Use the information on the following pages as a reference to know which fruit and veg are in season at any time of the year.

Spring

Spring is the beautiful time of year when all that is dormant starts to stir and come to life and the ground becomes awash with green. Spring produce is all about what is fresh and new. Highlights at this time of year include tangy rhubarb, buttery new potatoes and vibrant asparagus.

Fruit
- Rhubarb (we know it's technically a vegetable, but it tastes fruity!)
- Strawberries (late)

Vegetables
- Artichokes
- Asparagus (late)
- Aubergines (late)
- Beetroot
- Carrots (early/mid)
- Elderflowers (late)
- Kale (early)
- Leeks (early)
- Lettuce (late)
- New potatoes (late)
- Parsnips (early/mid)
- Peas (late)
- Purple sprouting broccoli (early)
- Radishes
- Rocket (mid/late)
- Spinach (mid/late)
- Spring greens
- Spring onions
- Sweetheart cabbage (late)
- Watercress

Spring recipes in this book
Spring Smoothie (page 38)
Spring Soup (page 70)
Bombay Potato Salad (page 78)

Summer

The bountiful summer months bring a wealth of delicious produce. Seasonal highlights include an abundance of berries and juicy, flavour-filled tomatoes.

Fruit
- Blackcurrants
- Blackberries (late)
- Blueberries (mid/late)
- Cherries
- Gooseberries (early/mid)
- Plums (late)
- Raspberries
- Rhubarb
- Strawberries

Vegetables
- Asparagus (early)
- Aubergines
- Beetroot
- Broad beans
- Broccoli (early/mid)
- Carrots (mid/late)
- Cauliflower (mid/late)
- Courgettes (early/mid)
- Cucumber (mid/late)
- Fennel (mid/late)
- Green beans (mid/late)
- Kale
- Leeks (late)
- Lettuces
- Mangetout (late)
- New potatoes (early/mid)
- Parsnips (late)
- Peas
- Peppers
- Potatoes (mid/late)
- Pumpkin (late)
- Radishes
- Rocket
- Runner beans
- Spring greens
- Spring onions
- Sweetcorn (late)
- Swiss chard
- Tomatoes (mid/late)
- Turnips
- Watercress
- White cabbage
- Wild mushrooms (late)

Summer recipes in this book
Summer Smoothie (page 38)
Hash Brown Breakfast Pizza (page 52)
Summer Soup (page 71)
Sweet Potato Salsa Salad (page 90)
Baked Ratatouille Rice (page 164)
Foolproof Focaccia (page 242)

Autumn

As the nights draw in and the days start to get colder, we start to crave warming bowls of soup and wonderfully pleasing puddings. Autumn has got your comfort-food cravings covered, with an abundance of pumpkins, squash and orchard fruits.

Fruit
- Apples (mid/late)
- Blackberries (early/mid)
- Cranberries (late)
- Pears
- Plums (early)
- Quinces (mid/late)
- Raspberries (early)
- Rhubarb
- Strawberries (early)

Vegetables
- Aubergines (early/mid)
- Beetroot
- Broccoli (early/mid)
- Brussels sprouts
- Carrots
- Cauliflowers
- Celeriac (mid/late)
- Celery
- Courgettes (early/mid)
- Cucumbers (early/mid)
- Jerusalem artichokes (late)
- Kale
- Leeks
- Lettuces (early/mid)
- Mangetout (early)
- Onions
- Parsnips
- Peas (early/mid)
- Peppers (early)
- Potatoes
- Pumpkin
- Radishes (early/mid)
- Red cabbage
- Rocket (early/mid)
- Runner beans (early/mid)
- Savoy cabbage (mid/late)
- Spinach (early/mid)
- Squash
- Swede (mid/late)
- Sweetcorn (early/mid)
- Tomatoes (early)
- Turnips
- Watercress (early)
- White cabbage
- Wild mushrooms

Autumn recipes in this book
Autumn Smoothie (page 39)
Apple Crumble Granola (page 42)
Autumn Soup (page 72)
Mushroom Stroganoff (page 178)
Ultimate Moussaka (page 184)
Apple Tarte Tatin (page 196)

Winter

The short, cold days of winter can seem too barren for much to grow, but there is plenty of delicious root veg in the ground for roasts, pies and stews. To add a punch of colour to the dark winter months, gloriously pink forced rhubarb has its short season here, too, and is well worth seeking out to use in warming pies and crumbles.

Fruit
- Apples
- Cranberries (early)
- Forced rhubarb (mid/late)
- Pears
- Quince (early)

Vegetables
- Beetroot
- Brussels sprouts
- Carrots
- Celeriac
- Celery
- Jerusalem artichokes
- Kale
- Leeks
- Onions
- Parsnips
- Potatoes
- Pumpkin
- Purple sprouting broccoli (late)
- Red cabbage
- Savoy cabbage
- Spring greens (mid/late)
- Spring onions (mid/late)
- Squash
- Swede
- Swiss chard
- Turnips
- Watercress
- White cabbage

Winter recipes in this book

MAKE RECIPES YOUR OWN

Perhaps the best way to keep food pocket-friendly is to tweak recipes to use up the produce you have in the fridge, rather than shopping for new ingredients. Cooking in this way will prevent waste, save you money and increase your confidence in the kitchen. Use the table below to work out cooking times for a range of produce. Try to keep your substitutions as close as possible to the ingredient suggested in the recipe and you can't go wrong!

Here is a basic guide to how to prep various varieties of veg. They're rough suggestions, not hard-and-fast rules, so take them with a pinch of salt (literally!), and always watch the food so you can see when it's ready.

Ingredient	Prep	Boil	Steam	Roast (200°C)	Grill	Shallow fry
Asparagus	Woody ends trimmed	3–5 minutes	3–5 minutes	10 minutes, lightly coated in oil	6 minutes, turning occasionally, lightly coated in oil	6 minutes, stirring occasionally, in a little oil
Aubergine	Cut into 1cm-thick slices	N/A	N/A	15 minutes, brushed generously with oil	8 minutes, turning once, brushed generously with oil	5–10 minutes, turning occasionally, in a generous amount of oil
Beetroot	Whole, trimmed but not peeled	30–40 minutes	30 minutes	40–60 minutes	N/A	N/A
Broccoli	Cut into small florets	5 minutes	5 minutes	10 minutes, lightly coated in oil	5–10 minutes, turning occasionally, lightly coated in oil	2–3 minutes, stirring occasionally, in a little oil

Brussels sprouts	Trimmed and outer leaves removed	5–10 minutes	6–8 minutes	20 minutes, lightly coated in oil	N/A	10 minutes, stirring occasionally, in a little oil
Butternut squash	Peeled and cut into 2.5cm cubes	7–10 minutes	10 minutes	25–30 minutes, lightly coated in oil	N/A	15 minutes, stirring occasionally, in a little oil
Carrots	Peeled and cut into bite-sized chunks	5–10 minutes	8–10 minutes	25–30 minutes, lightly coated in oil	N/A	10 minutes, stirring occasionally, in a little oil
Cauliflower	Cut into small florets	5 minutes	5 minutes	10 minutes, lightly coated in oil	5–10 minutes, turning occasionally, lightly coated in oil	2–3 minutes, stirring occasionally, in a little oil
Courgettes	Cut into 1cm-thick slices	5 minutes	5 minutes	15–20 minutes, lightly coated in oil	5 minutes, turning once, brushed with oil	5 minutes, stirring occasionally, in a little oil
Green beans	Trimmed	5 minutes	3–5 minutes	10–15 minutes, lightly coated in oil	N/A	5 minutes, stirring occasionally, in a little oil
Leeks	Trimmed and cut into 1cm-thick slices	N/A	5 minutes	10–15 minutes, lightly coated in oil	5 minutes, turning once, brushed with oil	10 minutes, stirring occasionally, in a little dairy-free butter
Potatoes	Peeled and cut into 2.5cm cubes	10–15 minutes	10–15 minutes	25–30 minutes, lightly coated in oil	N/A	15 minutes, stirring occasionally, in a little oil
Spinach	Leaves washed	30 seconds, until just wilted	2–3 minutes, until just wilted	N/A	N/A	1–2 minutes stirring occasionally, in a little water
Sweet potatoes	Peeled and cut into 2.5cm cubes	7–10 minutes	10 minutes	25–30 minutes, lightly coated in oil	N/A	10 minutes, stirring occasionally, in a little oil

COOKING ON A BUDGET

If you think about it, the raw ingredients in this book are all affordable – they're just plants! Eating veggie food only gets expensive the minute you begin adding shop-bought, factory-made products to your basket. Leave those out and you're already off to a great start. But budget cooking can still be difficult for a smorgasbord of reasons. The tips below will help you get back to basics, embrace plant-based eating head on and save yourself money in the process.

Cook from scratch

The biggest secret to cooking on a budget is to actually cook your food from scratch. Pre-prepared ingredients and ready meals may be great occasional time-savers, and definitely have their place, but we should cook for ourselves as much as we can. Making food from scratch with fresh ingredients is kinder to your health and your wallet, plus you get the satisfaction of knowing that you are responsible for all of the deliciousness on your plate. Likewise, meat replacement products are convenient and can taste great, but are often on the expensive side, so aside from the odd vegan sausage or cheeky block of tofu, we've tried to avoid them in this book.

Make a plan and stick to it!

Planning what to eat before you head to the supermarket is vital if you're looking to save money. Without a strategy you might fill your trolley with things you don't need, or buy expensive products because you're lacking inspiration. Make a list of the meals you want to eat during the week, check your cupboard for what you already have, then write a list of what you need to buy. Then, eyes focused straight ahead and ignoring the shiny packaging calling to you from the shelves, stick to the list! Online grocery shopping can take away a lot of the temptation you get being in an actual shop, so it can be a great way of making sure that you are only buying the things you actually need. Most supermarkets offer super-saver delivery slots for as little as £1; just be prepared to get up a little earlier than usual to answer the door!

Get the most out of herbs

Fresh herbs can deliver a punch of fragrant flavour that will bring any meal to life, but they have a short shelf life and can quickly turn from green and vibrant to brown and sad. To get the most out of them, unpack them straight away and stand them in a jar of water, much like you would a bunch of flowers. They will keep like this in the fridge for much longer than they would otherwise, and you can keep all your different types of herbs in the one container, just make sure to change the water every few days. If you have any outside space, or a spare windowsill, growing herbs in pots is a great way to have them on hand for very little cost. Pots of herbs are cheap to buy at supermarkets or garden centres and, looked after well, will give you an ever-replenishing supply of flavour at your fingertips.

Avoid decision fatigue

The idea of sitting down and leafing through your recipe books every week to make a meal plan may sound like a relaxing way to spend an hour or two, but in reality most of us don't have time to do this week after week. To avoid decision fatigue setting in, it's a good idea to plan to eat an old favourite at least a couple of nights a week. These are the simple, time-tested meals that we all have in our repertoire and turn to time and again when we don't have the mental energy to think of something

new and exciting to eat. We have different go-to meals: Henry loves a cheeky pesto pasta, any of the curries from this book, or a home-made pizza for a party; Ian's staples include hummus and Marmite on toast (or crumpets, see page 44), a wonderful roast dinner or a spag bol (but only on Tuesdays, don't ask!). These classics are much loved for a reason, so embrace them.

Perfectly imperfect

'Wonky' fruit and veg might not win any beauty contests, but they still taste wonderful and are a great way of saving a bit of money and making use of produce that would otherwise be wasted. Some supermarkets sell boxes of wonky veg cheaply and there are companies that work directly with farmers to package up imperfect seasonal fruit and veg and sell them directly to consumers in weekly or bi-weekly veg boxes. You won't have any control of what produce you receive, so they can be a false economy if you're someone who likes to know what's in their shopping basket, but if you're happy to adapt then they can be a great way of eating seasonally, saving a bit of money and preventing food waste all at the same time.

Waste not, want not

Once you've cooked a meal, you're often left with a collection of odds and ends: half a tin of tomatoes, the peelings from your veg or handfuls of herb stalks. Rather than throwing these away, they can become the building blocks for another meal. In this book we've tried to use up all the ingredients, but leftover herbs and veg peelings can be the base of a wonderfully flavourful veg stock (see page 234). When stored in cold water, they will also keep in the fridge for a week or so, so that you can keep adding to them until you have enough to cook with. Meanwhile, any half-used tins can be decanted into airtight containers and stored in the fridge for a few days until needed.

Raid your fridge

Before you do any shopping, have a look in your fridge and see what you already have to use up. If a recipe calls for carrots, but instead you have half a bag of parsnips in the veg drawer, throw these in instead. If we ask for fresh thyme but you've got an abundant rosemary bush in your garden, make the change. Recipes can be used as a jumping-off point and, as long as the flavours that you are swapping out are roughly comparable, the results should still be great. The chart on pages 20-21 will help you know how to change-up recipes, swap out ingredients and manage your cooking times.

Buy in bulk

In the world-food aisle of your local supermarket you'll find large bags of herbs, spices, pulses and grains that are cheaper by weight than buying smaller bags or glass jars. If you're going to be using an ingredient regularly and have the space to store it, these can be a great way of saving money and having a ready supply of a favourite ingredient. But don't go crazy – those big bags aren't the best option if you're only going to use an ingredient occasionally. First off, those big bags will take up space in your kitchen. But, also, longevity can vary – spices start to taste a bit dull after about a year, so if you're not going to use that enormous bag of cumin within 12 months, maybe get a small jar instead. Things like dried chickpeas and pulses are so much cheaper in bulk, and if you buy them dried they will keep for ages, some even say decades. Try our Ultimate Hummus (page 150), our Ultimate Chana Masala (page 130) and Superb Samosas (page 131) for great ways to use dried chickpeas.

BUDGET COOKING HACKS

Use the hacks below to get yourself into a budget-cooking mindset. We've given examples of a few recipes from this book to illustrate each hack, though skim through the pages and you'll see there are plenty more. Remember these hacks when planning your meals and you'll be saving money and reducing food waste in no time.

Don't let it go to waste

Give your veg scraps or any leftover herbs a whole new lease of life by cooking them into something new.

· Ian's Fridge-Raid Pesto Formula (page 231)
· Home-made Stocks (page 234)
· Foolproof Focaccia (page 242)

Two meals, one cook

Cook once but enjoy two delicious meals by quickly reinventing your leftovers.

· Tinned Tomato Soup & Tinned Tomato Pasta (pages 82-83)
· Big-Batch Bolognese Sauce (page 158) and Super-Easy Lasagne (page 159)
· Ian's Indian-style Shepherd's Pie (page 182), the filling for which also makes a delicious daal!

Make onions the star

Onions are miraculously cheap but are also sweet, delicious and sophisticated when cooked properly. Make the most of them with these dishes.

· Cheese & Onion Tarte Tatin (page 92)
· Shiro Wat and One-Day Injera (page 118)
· Thrifty Roast Dinner (page 168)

Adapt to the seasons

Change up your recipes to match the time of year.

· Seasonal Soups (pages 70-72)
· Seasonal Smoothies (pages 38-41)
· Overnight Oats (pages 47-49)

Use up your veg

Stop the sad-looking veg at the back of your fridge going to waste with these recipes.

· Ian's Fridge-Raid Pesto Formula (page 231)
· Veg Pakoras & Mixed Chutneys (page 114)
· Baked Ratatouille Rice (page 164)
· Tempura Crudités (page 112)
· Henry's Curry Stock (page 236)

Bulk with lentils and beans

Dried pulses are incredibly cheap and will sit waiting in your cupboard until needed. They are great for making a meal go further.

· Black Bean Soup & Chilli Cornbread (page 98)
· Ian's Indian-Style Shepherd's Pie (page 182)
· Big-Batch Bolognese Sauce (page 158)

Make it yourself

Make these storecupboard dishes from scratch to save money with added bragging rights.

· Apple Crumble Granola (page 42)
· Home-made Crumpets (page 44)
· Home-made Spreads (page 224)

Home-made basics

Develop skills and save money at the same time with these do-at-home basics.

· Lockdown Loaf (page 240)
· Home-made Tofu (page 222)
· Home-made Pasta (page 227)

Dried chickpeas for the win

These incredible recipes show just why dried chickpeas beat their tinned cousins, hands down. If you only try one recipe from this book, let it be Hummus with Mexican Beef.

· Hummus with Mexican Beef (page 151)
· Hummus Tabbouleh with Garlic Croûtons (page 152)
· Ultimate Chana Masala (page 130)

HOW TO BATCH COOK

Batch cooking is a great way of saving time and money, and it doesn't have to mean eating the same food over and over. With a little imagination, a batch-cooked base can be spun out in lots of different ways to make many different and exciting meals.

Making a double or triple portion of a meal is often proportionally not much more expensive than cooking it just once, so batching has become a firm money-saving favourite for us in the BOSH! kitchen. Good examples of recipes that use batching in this book are the Big-Batch Bolognese (page 158) and Henry's Curry Stock (page 236), both of which make far more than you will actually need for one meal but keep brilliantly in the freezer and can be quickly transformed into other tasty dishes. For example, having a portion of bolognese in the freezer means you can knock up our Super-Easy Lasagne (page 159) in a fraction of the time it would take to make it from scratch, while the stock forms the base for the Vindaloo, Balti and Madras recipes (pages 134–139). By being organised and making these batch elements ahead, you are opening up a whole world of possibilities. They are also easy to scale down, so if you don't want a huge batch or don't have space in your freezer to store it, simply halve the recipe.

If you are mostly cooking for a smaller crowd, most of the recipes in this book serve four, so if you avoid the call of double portions and simply save a portion or two then – hey presto! – you've got a meal ready for another day and saved a heap of time and money in the process.

When it comes to batching, your freezer is your best friend. We always try to keep ours at least a quarter empty so that we can see what's in there and have the space to add a few bits if needed. Clearly label anything that's ready to go in the freezer with the name of the dish and the date. Frozen food doesn't last indefinitely, so clearly labelling your dishes means that you can always use up the oldest items first. When packing up meals to freeze, always portion them into sizes that you're likely to eat in one meal. So if you're a two-person household, it makes far more sense to divide a big batch of something into two or four smaller portions.

We try to avoid using single-use plastic bags or cling film when packing things up for the freezer. Instead, we save plastic takeaway containers or invest in reusable silicone bags that can be used over and over. When storing food in a bag, squeeze out as much of the air as possible before sealing as that will save you space in the freezer and guard your food against freezer burn, which removes moisture from food and can affect the flavour.

STORECUPBOARD ESSENTIALS

When trying to cook on a budget, it can be useful to have a well-stocked pantry ready to dive into for essentials. These are the big-ticket items that are used in a lot of our recipes and that, once bought, will last for ages. It can be tempting to buy huge bags of herb and spices, but only do so if you have the space to store them and you are sure that you will get through them before they start to lose their flavour. A list of the items that we always have on hand in our cupboards is below.

Shopping list

Oils & vinegars

Oils: blended olive oil, extra-virgin olive oil, rapeseed oil, vegetable oil for frying
Vinegars: balsamic, cider, white wine

Dried herbs & spices

Spices: chilli flakes, chilli powder, cumin seeds, curry powder, fennel seeds, fenugreek seeds, garam masala, ground cinnamon, ground coriander, ground cumin, ground turmeric, nutmeg, paprika, pepper, smoked paprika, za'atar
Herbs: oregano, rosemary, thyme

Instant flavour hits

Savoury/spicy: mango chutney, Marmite, mustard, nutritional yeast, salt, soy sauce, sriracha, Tabasco, tahini, tomato purée
Sweet: Biscoff spread, cocoa powder, coffee, dark chocolate, golden syrup, maple syrup, peanut butter, vanilla extract

Tinned veg, grains, beans & pulses

Tinned veg: passata, sweetcorn, tinned tomatoes
Pasta & noodles: dried pasta shapes (wholewheat and white), lasagne sheets, rice vermicelli noodles, spaghetti, udon noodles, wholewheat noodles
Rice: basmati (brown and white), jasmine, pudding, risotto
Other grains: bulgur wheat, couscous, pearl barley, porridge oats
Beans & pulses: baked beans, black beans, chickpeas, haricot beans, kidney beans, lentils

Baking

Flours: gram (chickpea) flour, plain white, self-raising, strong bread flour (wholemeal and white), cornflour
Raising agents: baking powder, bicarbonate of soda, dried yeast, fast action yeast
Sweet: caster sugar, golden syrup, icing sugar, maple syrup, soft dark brown sugar
Nuts & seeds: almonds, cashews, hazelnuts, linseeds (flaxseeds), pecans, sesame seeds

Minimal equipment

If you're a keen cook, it can be tempting to fill your kitchen cupboards with expensive kit. But we know from experience that much of it will be rarely used and will sit gathering dust and taking up much-needed space. As an example, pasta makers are great, but unless you're going to be knocking up home-made pasta on a weekly basis, a rolling pin is a bit more work but will do the job. With some basic tools and a bit of elbow grease you can make any of the recipes in this book, so it's better to invest in a few good-quality items that will stand the test of time rather than buying every gadget going.

If you are going to invest in good-quality cookware, it's essential that you look after it well if you want it to last. Keep your knives sharp, your non-stick pans away from the kitchen scourer and keep a regular tally of where all the attachments for your food processor are (they're designed to save your time, so if you're spending 10 minutes looking for the right blade every time you need it, you may as well have chopped everything by hand). The list below contains all the essentials (and a few nice-to-haves) to get started with any of the recipes in this book.

- Sharp knives
- Chopping boards
- Whisk, spatula, tongs, wooden spoons and a ladle
- Range of non-stick frying pans and saucepans, including a large pot for batch cooking
- Colander and sieve
- Kitchen timer (a phone works brilliantly for this)
- Range of baking trays and roasting tins
- Large baking dish (for lasagne, moussaka, etc.)
- Lidded containers or reusable silicone bags for storing food in the fridge/freezer
- Stick or power blender
- Food processor with cutting blades (this will save you time, but is not essential)

BUDGET BANQUETS

Whether you want a romantic date-night spread, are cooking for a crowd or want to get some speedy lunches prepped and into the fridge for the week ahead, we've got you covered with these handy themed recipe collections.

BOSH! classics on a budget

Your BOSH! favourites, just as tasty, but kinder on the wallet.

· Big-Batch Bolognese Sauce (page 158)
· Super-Easy Lasagne (page 159)
· The No FOMO Burger (page 128)
· Fiery 5 Beans & Grains Chilli (page 162)
· Thai All-the-Greens Curry (page 186)
· Big BOSH! Breakfast Burgers (page 60)

Drinks & nibbles with friends

Keep the good times rolling with these bite-sized morsels that are great for sharing.

· Indian Spiced Cauliflower Wings (page 126)
· Teenie Tiny Tater Tots (page 154)
· Tempura Crudités (page 112)

Date-night dinners

Turn up the romance with a sophisticated date-night supper that is sure to impress.

· Winter Waldorf Salad (page 102)
· Sticky Teriyaki Aubergine (page 96)
· Chocolate Ganache Pots (page 210)

Dinner party dishes to impress

Be the host with the most with these brilliant dinner party centrepieces.

· Cheese & Onion Tarte Tatin (page 92)
· Henry's Mushroom & Nooch Risotto (page 180)
· Crispy Persian Fried Rice (page 121)
· Swedish Meatballs, Mash & Gravy (page 166)
· Frying Pan Biscoff Brownie (page 208)
· Mississippi Mud Pie (page 218)

Sunday lunch

See out the week in style with these great Sunday lunch options.

· Thrifty Roast Dinner (page 168)
· Ultimate Moussaka (page 184)
· Jane's Spanish Stew (page 174)
· Mushroom Stroganoff (page 178)
· Right Good Rice Pud (page 204)
· Apple Tarte Tatin (page 196)
· Salted Caramel Sticky Toffee Pudding
  (page 212)

Make-ahead weekday meals

Get organised for the week with these prep-ahead dinners.

· Apple Crumble Granola (page 42)
· Indian-Style Shepherd's Pie (page 182)
· Fiery 5 Beans & Grains Chilli (page 162)
· Swedish Meatballs, Mash & Gravy (page 166)
· Baked Ratatouille Rice (page 164)
· Take-a-Break Bakes (page 176)

Speedy weekday lunches

Whether you're working from home or want to whip up something quick to take to the office, we've got you covered with these make-ahead lunchtime feasts.

· Lemon Tofu (page 104)
· Carrot & Coriander Soup (page 76)
· Tinned Tomato Soup (page 82)
· Lockdown Curry Ramen (page 94)
· Vietnamese-style Noodle Salad (page 100)
· Ultimate Hummus (page 150)

Curry night classics

Throw a Friday-night curry feast for friends that's so much cheaper and better than a takeaway.

· Veg Pakoras & Mixed Chutneys (page 114)
· Chickpea Chaat Streetfood Bowl with Superb Samosas (page 132)
· Indian Spiced Cauliflower Wings (page 126)
· Mixed Veg Balti (page 134)
· Tofu Madras (page 136)
· Tempeh Vindaloo (page 138)

Summer barbecue

Make the burger crowd jealous with these moreish dishes that would go down brilliantly at a barbecue.

· Sweet Potato Salsa Salad (page 90)
· Sticky Teriyaki Aubergine (page 96)
· Aubergine Tandoori Drumsticks
  (page 148)

Street food favourites

Finger-licking dishes perfect for sharing.

· Bangin' Bao Buns (page 108)
· Jack's Wings & Fries (page 144)
· Tacos Acorazados (page 124)
· Aubergine Tandoori Drumsticks
  (page 148)
· The No FOMO Burger (page 128)

Picnic in the park

Make the most of the sunshine with these summery dishes that are perfect for transporting and eating al fresco.

· Bombay Potato Salad (page 78)
· Chunky Mushroom Turkish Pide (page 142)
· Healthy Doner Kebab (page 86)
· Ultimate Hummus (page 150)
· Chocolate Traycake (page 198)
· Lemon Drizzle Traycake (page 216)

BREAKFAST + BRUNCH

SEASONAL SMOOTHIES

Healthy and delicious, a smoothie is a brilliant way to start your day, at any time of the year. Here are four fantastic seasonal smoothies that are packed full of healthy fruit and veggies. Spring is all about gorgeous greens, for summer we've loaded up with brilliant berries, autumn's got loads of lush orchard fruits and for winter we've got root veg and zippy turmeric. Healthy eating never tasted so good!

SPRING

Serves 2 (about 500ml)

2 ripe kiwis
½ avocado
large handful of spinach leaves
1 large lime
200ml coconut water
2 tbsp sesame seeds
handful of ice cubes
maple syrup (optional)

Power blender

Peel the kiwis • Spoon the flesh of the avocado half into the blender and add the kiwis and spinach • Halve the lime and squeeze in the juice • Add the coconut water, half the sesame seeds and the ice cubes • Blend until smooth and thick • Taste, and sweeten a little if you like with a splash of maple syrup • Pour into glasses and sprinkle with the remaining sesame seeds

SUMMER

Serves 2 (about 500ml)

100g fresh strawberries
80g fresh raspberries
200ml oat milk
handful of ice cubes
1 small banana
2 tbsp rolled oats
1 tsp maple syrup (optional)

Power blender

Put two good-looking strawberries aside • Hull the rest and put them in the blender with the raspberries and half the oat milk • Add half of the ice cubes • Blend until smooth and then tip into glasses • Rinse the blender • Peel the banana and add it to the blender with the remaining oat milk, oats and the remaining ice cubes • Blend until smooth • Taste and sweeten with maple syrup if you like • Pour over the berry smoothie and gently stir to marble the mixture • Serve with a strawberry each

AUTUMN

Serves 2 (about 500ml)

2 tbsp almonds or almond butter
1 banana
1 ripe pear
1 tsp ground cinnamon, plus extra for dusting
handful of ice cubes
200ml almond milk
1 tsp maple syrup (optional)

Power blender • Frying pan on a high heat (optional)

If you're using whole almonds, tip them into the hot pan and cook for a few minutes until toasted, shaking the pan every now and then • Peel the banana and core the pear • Roughly chop them both and add to the blender • Add the cinnamon, ice cubes, almond milk and toasted almonds or almond butter and blend to a thick smoothie • Taste and sweeten with a splash of maple syrup if you like • Pour into glasses, dust with a little extra cinnamon and serve

WINTER

Serves 2 (about 500ml)

1 orange
1 carrot
1 apple
2cm piece fresh ginger
½ tsp ground turmeric
300ml apple juice
handful of ice cubes
1 tsp maple syrup (optional)

Power blender

Peel the orange and carrot • Peel and core the apple • Roughly chop all the fruit and add them to the blender • Peel the ginger and add it to the blender along with the turmeric • Pour in the apple juice and add the ice • Blend to a thick smoothie • Taste and sweeten if you like with a splash of maple syrup • Enjoy!

APPLE CRUMBLE GRANOLA

This hug-in-a-bowl breakfast tastes just like the ultimate comforting autumnal dessert! You can buy dried apple if you're in a hurry, but making your own is much more rewarding and cost-effective. This recipe makes a big batch that'll keep for a week in an airtight container. Serve it with ice-cold oat milk in the morning for a truly delicious breakfast or mid-afternoon for a hunger-busting snack!

Serves 12

50g golden syrup
75g caster sugar
pinch of salt
2 tsp ground cinnamon, plus extra for sprinkling
¼ tsp ground ginger
100ml olive oil
200g jumbo rolled oats
100g self-raising flour (or 100g plain flour and ½ tsp baking powder)
175g nuts (we used hazelnuts and blanched almonds)
75g pumpkin seeds
125g raisins or sultanas

For the dried apples
1 lemon
100ml water
4 medium apples

To serve
dairy-free milk
dairy-free yoghurt

The night before: Preheat the oven to 80°C · 2 or 3 wire oven racks

In the morning: Preheat the oven to 160°C · Small saucepan · 1 large or 2 medium roasting tins · Spatula or butter knife

Make the dried apples · The night before you want to eat your granola, halve the lemon and squeeze the juice into a bowl · Add the water · Core and thinly slice the apples into 5mm rounds and toss them in the lemon water · Space out the slices on the wire racks and put them in the warm oven to dry out for 1 hour, propping the door open with a wooden spoon so that steam can escape · After an hour, reduce the temperature to 70°C and close the door · Leave for 1½–2 hours, until the apples are dry but slightly spongy with an even texture · Leave to cool at room temperature and then roughly tear a few to vary the size of the pieces · Store in an airtight container with a few grains of rice at the bottom to soak up any excess moisture

Prepare the granola · The next morning, preheat the oven · Place the small saucepan over a low heat · Add the syrup, sugar, salt, spices and oil and melt for 2 minutes, stirring all the time · Tip about a third of the mixture into a roasting tin · Tip half the oats into the tin and mix well to coat the oats evenly in the syrup mixture · Tip the rest of the oats into the saucepan along with the flour and the rest of the sugar mixture · Use a spatula or butter knife to combine, but don't over-mix · Tip clumps of the mixture into the roasting tin or tins, trying not to crowd the tin · Spread everything out evenly

Bake the granola · Bake in the hot oven for 15 minutes · Roughly chop the nuts · Remove the tray from the oven, mix up the oats and break up the clumps a little · Reduce the heat to 140°C · Fold in the nuts and seeds and return to the oven to bake for another 15 minutes · Leave to cool for about 30 minutes before adding the raisins or sultanas

Serve · Spoon the granola into bowls and top with dairy-free yoghurt, milk, some dried apple slices and a sprinkling of cinnamon · Store any remaining granola in an airtight container

HOME-MADE CRUMPETS

You can buy crumpets really easily but making your own is way more rewarding. You don't need fancy crumpet rings for this recipe, simply use an empty can with the top and bottom removed for a budget-friendly hack that works just as well. Try our toppings over the page – the hummus and Marmite combo might sound odd, but trust us, it's a revelation!

Makes 8 crumpets
Serves 4

250g bread flour
2 x 7g sachets fast-action
    dried yeast
½ tsp caster sugar
½ tsp bicarbonate
    of soda
300ml warm water
6 tbsp vegetable or
    sunflower oil,
    for frying
1 x topping of your choice
    (see overleaf)

Clean tea towel · Large frying pan · 8–10cm metal cookie cutter (or use shallow tin cans with the top and bottom removed)

Make the crumpet mix · Put the flour, yeast, sugar, bicarbonate of soda and water in a large bowl and mix to combine · Cover and leave to rest for 15 minutes

Cook the crumpets · Put the frying pan over a medium-low heat and brush it with oil · Pour the oil for frying into a shallow bowl · Dip your moulds into the bowl and brush around them with oil, then place them in the pan · Add enough batter to each mould to come about halfway up the sides (about 1cm deep if using a tin) being careful not to overfill them as the crumpets will rise a lot · Cook for 5 minutes, until the bubbles that appear on the top have burst · If you're using a tin, carefully release the crumpet by running a knife around the inside edge of the tin, being careful not to burn your hands as the metal will be hot · Flip over the crumpets to cook the other sides for another minute · Transfer the cooked crumpets to a board, sliding them out of the moulds, if using · Repeat as necessary until you have made 8 crumpets

Add the toppings · Add your chosen topping (see overleaf) and serve straightaway · Store any leftover crumpets in a sealed container and toast before eating

CRUMPET TOPPINGS

AVOCADO, LIME & SESAME

Makes enough for 8 crumpets

1 large avocado
½ lime
pinch of salt
pinch of black pepper
sesame seeds (black if you
    can find them)

Halve and carefully stone the avocado by tapping the stone firmly with the heel of a knife so that it lodges in the pit, then twist and remove • Scoop the flesh into a bowl • Squeeze over the lime juice and sprinkle with the salt and pepper • Mix well to combine • Spread the mixture on to the crumpets and sprinkle with some sesame seeds

PEANUT BUTTER & HOME-MADE JAM

Makes enough for 8 crumpets

200g fresh raspberries
100g sugar
½ lemon
4 tbsp peanut butter

Small saucepan • Sterilise a jar and lid by washing them in hot soapy water and then filling them to the top with boiling water, then drain on a clean tea towel until completely dry

Tip the raspberries and sugar into the saucepan • Squeeze in the lemon juice • Place over a medium heat and cook for a couple of minutes, stirring until the sugar has dissolved, then turn up the heat and bring to the boil • Boil for 6–8 minutes, stirring now and then so that it doesn't catch • Take the pan off the heat and mash the raspberries a bit to create a thick jam • Carefully tip into the sterilised jar, put the lid on and leave to cool • Spread the crumpets with peanut butter and top with the home-made jam

MARMITE, HUMMUS & SPROUTS

Makes enough for 8 crumpets

4 tbsp hummus
4 tsp Marmite
40g broccoli sprouts, cress
    or micro herbs

Spread the crumpets with the hummus and then the Marmite • Sprinkle over a handful of sprouts, cress or micro herbs and serve

OVERNIGHT OATS

Overnight oats are such a no-brainer. They're healthy, taste great and can be thrown together the night before, ready for a quick grab-and-go breakfast in the morning. We've treated you to four different versions here, so you can keep your breakfast interesting for most of the week!

Serves 1

50g rolled oats
125ml dairy-free milk
1 x flavour combo of your
        choice (see over page)

Start the night before you want to eat your oats • Container such as a clean jam jar • Blender or stick blender and a small saucepan if you're making super carrot cake flavour • Blender or stick blender and frying pan if you're making chocolate flavour

Make the base • Mix the oats with the milk • Add a pinch of salt and sugar if you like • Set aside while you prepare your chosen flavour

CHOCOLATE

35g pumpkin seeds
½ avocado
2 tbsp syrup
15–20g cocoa powder,
    plus extra for dusting
50ml dairy-free milk
20g desiccated coconut
60g blueberries

Place a frying pan over a high heat • Scatter over the pumpkin seeds and cook for a few minutes until toasted, shaking the pan every now and then • Spoon the avocado half into a blender or bowl • Add the syrup, cocoa powder, 20g of the pumpkin seeds and 50ml milk • Blend until smooth • Spoon a layer of the mixture into the container and layer up with the coconut, blueberries, pumpkin seeds and the oat mixture • Leave to rest in the fridge overnight • Sprinkle the rest of the toasted seeds over the top and dust with a little more cocoa

BERRY

100g fresh strawberries
50g frozen berries
2 tbsp maple syrup
2 tbsp shop-bought granola

Slice the strawberries and tip half into a bowl • Add the frozen berries and the maple syrup and stir to coat the berries in the syrup • Layer up the berries and the oat mixture in the container • Leave to rest in the fridge overnight • Top with the rest of the strawberries and the granola

SUPER CARROT CAKE

1 small carrot (about 70g)
1 small banana
1 small piece of fresh
    turmeric (or ¼ tsp ground)
50g walnuts
½–1 tsp ground
    cinnamon, plus extra for dusting
pinch of black pepper
60g blueberries
1½ tbsp chia seeds
maple syrup, to drizzle

Peel and slice the carrot • Bring a pan of water
to the boil, add the carrots and cook for 8
minutes • Drain and cool • Peel the banana
and break it into chunks • Peel and grate the
fresh turmeric, if using • Roughly chop the
walnuts • Add the banana, carrots, fresh or
ground turmeric, cinnamon, pepper and half
the walnuts to a blender or jug and blend until
smooth • Layer up the mixture in the container
with the oat mixture, blueberries and chia
seeds • Repeat until you've used up all the
oats and carrot mixture and half the remaining
walnuts and chia seeds • Leave to rest in
the fridge overnight • Sprinkle the reserved
walnuts, chia seeds and syrup over the top and
dust with a pinch of cinnamon

PEANUT BUTTER

½ large apple
1 tsp lemon juice
½ tsp ground cinnamon,
    plus extra for sprinkling
2 tbsp maple syrup
2 heaped tbsp crunchy
    peanut butter, plus extra for drizzling

Core and thinly slice the apple • Put the
slices into a bowl and add the lemon juice,
½ teaspoon cinnamon and the maple syrup •
Toss to coat • Layer up the apples, oats and
peanut butter in the container • Leave to rest
in the fridge overnight • Top with a last dollop
of peanut butter and a pinch of cinnamon

ULTIMATE CINNAMON ROLLS

The delightful aroma of these beauties wafting out of the oven will get your taste buds firing, for sure. For a brilliant get-ahead hack, you can make these up until the rolls are formed and in their tin and then cover them and put them in the fridge to slowly rise overnight. The next morning, just pop them in a preheated oven and, voila! A tasty way to start your day.

Makes 9

For the dough
200ml oat milk
115g dairy-free butter
2 tbsp caster sugar
1 x 7g sachet yeast
250g strong white
    bread flour
250g plain flour
½ tbsp salt
1 tbsp apple cider vinegar

For the filling
100g dairy-free butter
75g light brown sugar
2 tbsp cinnamon
pinch of salt

For the icing
200g icing sugar
2–3 tbsp water

Clear a shelf in the oven • Grease a 20cm cake tin with dairy-free butter • Small saucepan over a medium heat • Large bowl • Rolling pin

Make the dough • Pour the oat milk into the saucepan and heat until steaming • Take off the heat, add the dairy-free butter and stir until melted • Stir in the sugar and yeast and set aside • Mix the flours and salt together in the large bowl • Make a well in the centre and add the oat-milk mixture • Add the apple cider vinegar and mix to make a soft dough • Tip on to a clean work surface and knead until smooth and elastic • Clean the bowl and place the dough back inside, cover with a clean cloth and set aside for 1–1½ hours, until doubled in size

Make the filling • Put all the filling ingredients into a bowl and whisk until light and fluffy • Set aside

Prepare the rolls • Tip the dough on to a clean work surface dusted liberally with flour and roll it into a large rectangle about 30 x 25cm • Spread the filling evenly over the pastry • Starting at the longest edge, roll the pastry into a log • Slice into 9 equal circles, then lay each slice on its side • Take the last 2cm of each roll and tuck it underneath the pastry • Arrange the rolls in the cake tin, leaving a little space between each one • Cover and leave to rise for another 30–40 minutes, until risen and puffy • Preheat the oven to 180°C

Bake • Bake the rolls for 20–30 minutes, until golden • Remove and set aside to cool in the tin

Ice the rolls • Put the icing sugar into a bowl and gradually mix in enough of the water to make a drizzle • Remove the cooled rolls from the tin, drizzle with the icing and leave to set before serving

HASH BROWN BREAKFAST PIZZA

This is the kind of weekend breakfast that's almost worth getting a hangover for. The pizza base is a massive crispy hash brown and the toppings are everything you'd expect to see on a breakfast plate. The secret to getting your base golden and crunchy is to give the grated potato a really good squeeze to get rid of any excess moisture, so be sure not to miss that step.

Serves 4

100g plain flour
½ tsp salt
1 tsp baking powder
450g floury potatoes
1 medium onion
3 tbsp cooking oil

For the topping
15 cherry tomatoes
a few sprigs fresh thyme
    or 1 tsp dried
2½ tbsp light olive oil
1 tsp caster sugar
250g button mushrooms
3 garlic cloves
100g frozen whole
    leaf spinach
salt and black pepper

To serve
1 x 400g tin baked
    beans (optional)
brown sauce or ketchup

Preheat the oven to 160°C • Clean tea towel • Medium frying pan • Large baking sheet • Small saucepan of cold water

Make the hash • Measure the flour, salt and baking powder into a bowl • Coarsely grate the potatoes into the middle of the clean tea towel • Peel and finely slice the onion and pile it over the potatoes • Bring up the corners of the towel and squeeze out as much liquid as you can into the sink • Tip the potatoes and onions into the flour bowl • Mix well to coat

Cook the hash • Heat 1 tablespoon of the oil in a medium frying pan over a medium heat • Add the hash brown mixture, roughly spreading it to the edges with the fork but trying not to compact it too much • Cook for 10 minutes

Meanwhile, prep the toppings • Halve the tomatoes and put them in a bowl • Pick the thyme leaves if needed • Drizzle the tomatoes with ½ tablespoon of the oil and sprinkle over the sugar, thyme and some salt and pepper • Toss to coat • Halve any larger mushrooms

Flip the hash • Take the pan off the heat • Lay a board over the pan and flip the hash on to it • Add another tablespoon of oil to the pan and slide the hash back into it • Cook for another 10 minutes • Slide the hash on to the baking sheet and transfer it to the oven • Bake for 20 minutes

Cook the toppings • Once the hash has been in the oven for 5 minutes, add the tomatoes, cut-side down, to one side of the baking tray • Roast for the remaining 15 minutes • Peel and finely slice the garlic • Wipe out the frying pan and place it over a medium-high heat • Add a tablespoon of oil • Add the mushrooms and some salt, and pepper and cook for 10 minutes • Add the garlic for the final 5 minutes, stirring now and then, until the mushrooms are golden and almost cooked through • Meanwhile, put the spinach into the pan of cold water and set it over a medium heat • Bring to the boil and then drain the spinach, squeezing out excess water with a spoon • If using, tip the baked beans into the pan and place it over a medium heat to warm through

Top the pizza • Take the tray from the oven and top the hash with the drained spinach, roasted tomatoes and their juices, and the mushrooms • Drizzle your favourite sauces over the top and serve with the warm beans on the side, if you like

PULP FICTION BLUEBERRY PANCAKES

These are the kind of indecently delicious, beautifully fluffy diner-style pancakes that you normally only see in American movies. Slathered in yoghurt, topped with juicy fresh blueberries and dripping with maple syrup, these really are a thing of beauty. Tarantino would be proud, Honey Bunny.

Serves 4

150g self-raising flour
2½ tbsp (30g)
    caster sugar
1 tsp baking powder
good pinch of sea salt
180ml dairy-free milk
½ tsp vanilla extract
150g blueberries (fresh
    or frozen)
4 tbsp sunflower or
    vegetable oil

To serve
4 tbsp maple syrup
4 tbsp dairy-free yoghurt
toasted nuts (optional)

Preheat oven to 100°C and put a large plate inside to warm • Large non-stick frying pan over a medium heat

Make the batter • Put the flour, sugar, baking powder and salt into a bowl and mix to combine • Slowly add the dairy-free milk and whisk to a smooth batter • Stir in the vanilla and half the blueberries • If you're using frozen blueberries, leave the remaining berries out to thaw a little

Make the pancakes • Add a tablespoon of the oil to the hot pan • Spoon 4 heaped tablespoons of the batter into the pan, spacing them out evenly • Cook for 3–5 minutes, until bubbles appear on top and the pancakes are browned on the bottom • Flip and cook for another 3 minutes • Transfer to the warm plate in the oven • Repeat to use up all the pancake mixture

Serve • Stack 2 or 3 pancakes on each plate • Top each one with a spoonful of yoghurt and a scattering of berries • Finish with a drizzle of maple syrup and a handful of toasted nuts, if using

APPLE & CINNAMON FRENCH TOAST

Super-easy to make and absolutely delicious, we're convinced this is the only recipe for vegan French toast you'll ever need. The cinnamon sugar and maple-roasted apples make it the perfect breakfast for a lazy Saturday morning. Give it a whirl – you won't be disappointed!

Serves 4

3 tbsp dairy-free butter
4 thick slices crusty
    bread, preferably
    2–3 days old

For the maple-roasted apples
1 apple
2 tbsp maple syrup
½ tsp ground cinnamon
1 tbsp water
¼ lemon

For the cinnamon sugar
25g caster sugar
¼ tbsp ground cinnamon

For the batter
125ml oat milk
30g cornflour
1 tsp caster sugar
1 tsp ground flaxseeds
½ tsp baking powder
½ tsp ground cinnamon

To serve
a handful of nuts
dairy-free pouring cream

Line a small roasting tin with parchment paper • Baking tray • Large frying pan

Toast the nuts • Spread the nuts over the baking tray and place it in the cold oven • Turn the heat to 200°C and remove the tray after 10–15 minutes, once the nuts are toasted • Leave to cool slightly and then roughly chop

Roast the apples • Core the apple and cut it into eighths • Lay the slices in the roasting tin • Sprinkle over the maple syrup, cinnamon, water and the juice of the lemon and mix everything together • Roast in the hot oven for 15–20 minutes, until softened

Make the cinnamon sugar • Combine the cinnamon and sugar in a bowl and then spread evenly over a plate

Make the batter • Add all the ingredients for the batter to a large bowl and mix well

Toast the bread slices • Place the frying pan over a medium heat and melt the dairy-free butter • Lay a slice of bread in the batter for 2–3 seconds, then flip it over and leave it for another 2–3 seconds • Transfer to the frying pan • Repeat with the remaining slices so you have them all in one pan (you may have to do this in batches) • Flip the slices after about 3 minutes and fry until both sides are crisp and golden

Prepare the plates • Transfer the slices to a chopping board and cut them in half • Lay the halves in the cinnamon sugar and dust them all over • Transfer to plates, top with the roasted apples, drizzle over some dairy-free cream and scatter over the toasted, chopped nuts • Serve immediately

SUPER COULIS YOGHURT POTS

A light and healthy breakfast that looks and tastes like a cheesecake sounds too good to be true, right? Well it isn't. It's true! You can buy shop-bought granola or make the Apple Crumble Granola from page 42, but leave out the apples. We like these yoghurt pots so much we reckon they'd work perfectly as a dessert after a light summer dinner.

Makes 5

250g granola (see
    page 42)
500g dairy-free yoghurt
100g fresh mixed berries
1–2 bananas (optional)

For the coulis

300g frozen mixed
    berries
3 tbsp caster sugar
1 tsp lemon juice
½ tbsp cornflour
1 tbsp water

Saucepan on a medium heat • Glass tumblers

Make the coulis • Add the frozen berries, sugar and lemon juice to the saucepan and stir for 10 minutes until the berries have thawed out completely and are starting to break down • Take the pan off the heat • Mix the cornflour and water together in a small bowl to form a slurry • Add the slurry to the pan, stir to mix and leave to cool a little • Transfer to a container and leave to cool for 10 minutes before putting it into the fridge to cool completely

Build the yoghurt pots • Tip 50g of granola into the bottom of each tumbler • Top with 100g yoghurt • Peel and chop the banana and divide it between the glasses • Drizzle the coulis over the top • Dress the pots with the fresh berries and serve immediately

BIG BOSH! BREAKFAST BURGERS

Burger for breakfast. Sounds like a great idea, right? These are naughty, indulgent and utterly delicious - the perfect thing to rustle up for you and your mates the morning after the night before. Ronald ain't got nothing on us. BOSH!

Serves 4

6 plant-based sausages, at room temperature
1 small garlic clove
1 tsp black pepper
2 tsp dried sage
½ tsp dried thyme
½ tsp fennel seeds
pinch of nutmeg
4 slices dairy-free American-style cheese
a little oil, for greasing

For the 'bacon' mushrooms

250g closed-cup or chestnut mushrooms
1½ tbsp soy sauce
1½ tbsp maple syrup
1½ tbsp apple cider vinegar
1 tbsp olive oil

For the tofu 'egg'

280g firm tofu
3 tbsp vegetable oil, plus more for frying
½ tbsp ground turmeric
½ tsp black pepper
½ tsp garlic powder
½ tsp onion powder

To serve

4 English muffins
4 tbsp dairy-free butter
tomato ketchup or brown sauce

Preheat the oven to 180°C • Line 2 baking trays • Tofu press or 2 clean tea towels and a weight • Large frying pan • Toaster or grill heated to max

Prepare the tofu • Press the tofu for 10 minutes using a tofu press or place it between two clean tea towels, lay it on a plate and put a weight on top

Make the burger patties • Place the plant-based sausages in a mixing bowl and mash with a fork • Peel the garlic and grate it into the bowl • Crack the pepper • Add the dried herbs and spices and stir to combine • Taste and adjust the seasoning as needed • Grease your hands with a little oil and shape the mixture into 4 burger patties that are the same diameter as the muffins • Place on one of the baking trays and roast in the hot oven for 18 minutes • Remove the tray and place a slice of dairy-free cheese on top of each patty • Return to the oven for another 2 minutes

Meanwhile, make the 'bacon' mushrooms • Slice the mushrooms • Mix the soy sauce, maple syrup and apple cider vinegar in a bowl • Add the mushrooms and stir to coat in the marinade • Spread the mushrooms out over a baking tray, drizzle the oil over the top, then roast for 18–20 minutes

Make the tofu 'egg' • Put the pressed tofu on its side and cut it into 4 thin slices, then carefully trim the corners to make the slices roughly the same size as the muffins • Mix the 3 tablespoons of vegetable oil and the remaining ingredients together on a plate • Move the slices of tofu around in the marinade to coat • Put a frying pan over a medium heat and warm a couple of tablespoons of oil • Fry the tofu slices for 3 minutes on each side, until the edges are turning golden brown

Prepare the muffins • Halve the muffins and toast until golden and crispy • Butter the slices

Build the burgers • Place the cheese-topped burger patties on the muffin bases • Lay a tofu egg on top of each patty (you may need to trim the corners a little bit to get a nice round burger shape!) • Top with the bacon mushrooms, ketchup or brown sauce and the muffin tops • Serve immediately

SATURDAY MORNING CRÊPES

Henry and his family used to love French-style crêpes as an occasional decadent weekend breakfast, so we decided to veganise them, so that you can enjoy them too! We've included three awesome toppings for you to try. Each one makes enough for all the crêpes, so pick your favourite and go nuts!

Makes 10 crêpes

275g plain flour
525ml dairy-free milk
2 tbsp caster sugar
3 tbsp vegetable oil
1 x topping of your choice
   (see opposite)

Preheat the oven to 100°C and put a plate inside to warm • **Blender or whisk** • **Wide shallow frying pan**

Make the batter • Measure the flour, milk, sugar and 1 tablespoon of the oil into a bowl or blender • Whisk or blend until completely smooth • Leave to rest for 10 minutes while you prepare your topping

Cook the crêpes • Use a little of the remaining oil to grease the inside of the pan • Set the pan over a medium heat • Once hot, pour half a ladleful of batter into the middle of the pan • Tilt the pan to spread the batter evenly over the base • After 2–3 minutes, when the crêpe starts to brown around the edges and the bottom is firm and golden, flip it over and cook for a further 2 minutes • Transfer to the plate in the oven to keep warm • Repeat to make 10 crêpes • Top with your topping of choice and enjoy!

BANOFFEE

Makes enough for 10 crêpes

4 medium bananas
75g light brown sugar
75g dairy-free butter
50ml golden or maple syrup
2 tsp vanilla extract
80g Biscoff spread
dairy-free yoghurt

Blender

Peel 2 of the bananas and place them in the blender • Add the light brown sugar, dairy-free butter, syrup, vanilla and Biscoff • Blend for about 2 minutes, until completely smooth • Peel and slice the remaining bananas • To serve your banoffee crêpes, spread them with the sauce, top with sliced bananas, drizzle over a little dairy-free yoghurt and serve immediately

CHOCOLATE

Makes enough for 10 crêpes

50g dark chocolate
270ml whippable dairy-free
   double cream
90g dairy-free milk chocolate
100g mixed nuts and raisins

Microwavable bowl or small saucepan

Finely chop the dark chocolate • Pour 90ml of the dairy-free cream into a microwavable bowl and heat in the microwave until very hot (3 x 30-second bursts at full power should do it), or pour into a small saucepan and place over a medium heat) • Add all the chocolate to the bowl and leave to stand for 1 minute before stirring the chocolate into the cream • Set aside for 20 minutes • Pour the remaining cream into a separate bowl • Whisk until well whipped and firmed up • To serve your chocolate crêpes, spread them with the chocolate sauce, dollop on a little whipped cream and top with mixed nuts and raisins

FRUITY

Makes enough for 10 crêpes

270ml whippable dairy-free
   double cream
400g fresh rhubarb
300g fresh strawberries
1 star anise
75g caster sugar
2 tsp vanilla extract

Whisk • Medium saucepan

Pour the dairy-free cream into a bowl • Whisk until well whipped and firmed up • Put the bowl in the fridge • Trim the rhubarb and cut it into 3cm lengths • Hull and halve the strawberries • Add the rhubarb, sugar, vanilla and star anise to the pan • Place over a low heat and cook until the fruit is softened but still holding its shape, about 5–10 minutes • Remove the star anise from the rhubarb, add the strawberries and gently toss to combine • To serve your fruity crêpes, spoon over the rhubarb and strawberries and top with whipped cream

IAN'S SIMPLE SHAKSHUKA

We've put this in the brunch chapter as it's a great start to the day, but shakshuka makes a wonderful meal at any time. Served with toasted pitta for dunking, this silky red pepper stew feels really warming and generous. And we're chuffed with these vegan eggs; they look awesome and the flavour is fantastic. Super fun and perfect for Instagram!

Serves 2

1 red pepper
2 tbsp olive oil
1 large white onion
1 fresh red chilli
3 garlic cloves
handful fresh coriander
1 tsp dried oregano
1 tsp ground cumin
1 tsp smoked
    sweet paprika
½ tsp ras el hanout
1½ tbsp tomato purée
1 tsp caster sugar
1 tbsp red wine vinegar
1 x 400g tin
    chopped tomatoes
2 bay leaves
1 cinnamon stick
salt

For the 'egg yolks'
½ yellow pepper
½ tbsp plant-based mayo
1 heaped tsp tahini
½ lemon
salt

For the 'egg whites'
4 tbsp dairy-free yoghurt
½ lemon
salt

To serve
1 spring onion
4 pitta breads

Large frying pan • Power blender

Blacken the peppers • Light your largest gas ring or preheat your grill to high • Put the red and yellow peppers directly on the flame or under the grill for 10–15 minutes, turning them every 5 minutes, until blackened on all sides • Set aside in a bowl to cool and steam with a plate over the top

Cook the vegetables • Place the frying pan over a medium heat and pour in the olive oil • Peel and finely chop the onion and add it to the pan • Halve the chilli, dice one half and finely slice the other • Peel and grate the garlic cloves • Add the diced chilli and garlic to the pan and stir, cooking for 5 minutes • Finely chop the coriander stems and add them to the pan, reserving the leaves • Add the oregano and the spices • Stir and cook for another 5 minutes • Add the tomato purée and sugar and stir for 5–10 minutes, until the mixture is getting darker and sticky • Add the vinegar to the pan and let it bubble away and evaporate • Add the tinned tomatoes, bay leaves and cinnamon and a good splash of water and leave to simmer for 8–10 minutes, until thickened and combined • Lower the heat and keep warm until needed

Peel the peppers • Rub the burned skin from the cooled peppers with your fingers • Seed and roughly chop the peppers • Add the red pepper to the shakshuka • Put the yellow pepper in the blender

Make the 'egg yolk' • Add the plant-based mayo and tahini to the blender with the yellow pepper • Squeeze in the juice of the lemon and season with salt • Blend to a paste

Make the 'egg white' • Put the yoghurt in a bowl • Squeeze in the juice of the lemon and season with salt • Mix to combine

Finish the shakshuka • Remove the bay and cinnamon sticks from the pan • Taste the shakshuka and adjust the seasoning if necessary • If it looks dry, add a splash of water and stir it in • Make sure it's nice and warm • Press the back of a spoon into the mixture to make 4 wells • Spoon a tablespoon of the 'egg white' into each well • Use a teaspoon to add a spoonful of the 'egg yolk' into the centre of each white

Serve • Grill or toast the pittas • Scatter the reserved coriander leaves over the shakshuka • Finely slice the spring onion and scatter it over along with the sliced red chilli • Serve the pittas alongside for dipping

SOUPS, SALADS + LIGHT MEALS

SEASONAL SOUPS

Soup and crusty bread is one of our all-time favourite meals and these soups are truly incredible. Here we have four fantastic seasonal recipes that will keep you happy all year round. For spring we've gone fresh and fragrant, our summer soup is chilled to keep you cool, autumn is all about earthiness and the winter version is super hearty. Each one's an absolute belter, so take your pick and enjoy..

SPRING SOUP

Serves 4–6

1 large onion
250g asparagus
1 large courgette
1 tbsp olive oil
2 garlic cloves
1 tbsp fennel seeds
1 litre vegetable stock
small bunch of fresh mint
small bunch of fresh basil
350g fresh or frozen peas
salt and black pepper
extra-virgin olive oil,
    for drizzling

For the croûtons
2 pitta breads
1 tbsp olive oil
1 tsp dried oregano
big pinch of salt

Preheat the oven to 180°C • Baking tray • Large saucepan with a lid over a medium heat • Power or stick blender

Make the croûtons • Tear the pitta into 2cm chunks • Add to the baking tray and sprinkle with the olive oil, oregano and salt • Toss well and roast for 10 minutes until golden and crisp

Make the soup • Peel and finely chop the onion • Trim and roughly chop the asparagus and courgette • Pour the olive oil into the hot saucepan, add the onion and fry for 5 minutes, until softened • Peel and roughly chop the garlic and add it to the pan along with the fennel seeds and chopped vegetables • Cook for 5 minutes, stirring • Add the stock, cover and cook for 10 minutes, until the vegetables are softened • Separate the leaves from the herbs and add most of them to the soup • Add the peas, bring to the boil and cook for 1 minute • Remove from the heat • Blitz to a smooth soup in the pan or blender • Taste and season

Serve • Ladle into bowls • Scatter with croûtons and top with the remaining herbs and a drizzle of extra-virgin olive oil

SUMMER SOUP

Serves 4–6

100g blanched almonds
1 large white onion
2 tbsp olive oil, plus extra for drizzling
big pinch of salt
small bunch of fresh parsley
2 large cucumbers
2 garlic cloves
1 litre vegetable stock
small bunch of fresh chives
3 celery sticks
1½ lemons
200ml dairy-free yoghurt
salt and black pepper

Small frying pan over a medium heat • Large saucepan over a medium heat • Power or stick blender

Toast the almonds • Tip the blanched almonds into the hot frying pan and toast for a couple of minutes, shaking the pan occasionally, until golden • Take the pan off the heat

Make the soup • Peel and finely chop the onion • Pour the oil into the hot saucepan • Add the onion and a big pinch of salt • Fry for 5 minutes, until soft • Pick the parsley leaves and put them to one side • Finely chop the stems • Roughly chop the cucumbers • Peel and roughly chop the garlic • Add the garlic and chopped parsley stems to the pan • Cook for 1 minute • Add the cucumber • Cook for 5 minutes • Add the stock and three-quarters of the toasted almonds • Bring to the boil and cook for 10 minutes, then remove from the heat • Add the chives and most of the parsley tops, reserving a few for garnish • Set aside to cool to room temperature • Blend in the pan or blender until very smooth • Trim and roughly chop 2 of the celery stalks and add them to the soup • Squeeze in the juice of the half lemon • Season generously and blend until smooth and creamy • Stir in half the yoghurt • Taste and add more lemon juice to taste • Tip into a container and refrigerate until cool

Serve • Roughly chop the remaining almonds and finely slice the remaining celery stick • Ladle the soup into bowls and drizzle with olive oil • Sprinkle over the chopped almonds and celery slices • Scatter with a few parsley leaves and serve

AUTUMN SOUP

Serves 4–6

1 large red onion
1kg cooked beetroot
2 fresh red chillies
2 tbsp olive oil
2 garlic cloves
1 tbsp cumin seeds
1 litre vegetable stock
dairy-free yoghurt
fresh dill, for garnish
salt and black pepper
crusty bread, to serve

For the spiced pumpkin seeds
4 tbsp pumpkin seeds
1 tbsp cumin seeds
olive oil

**Large saucepan with a lid over a medium heat •
Small frying pan • Power or stick blender**

Make the soup • Peel and finely chop the
onion • Peel and roughly chop the beetroot
• Trim and seed the chillies if you don't like
your soup too spicy • Finely chop one and
finely slice the other • Pour the oil into the
hot saucepan • Add the onion and fry for
5 minutes, until softened • Peel and roughly
chop the garlic and add it to the pan along
with the cumin seeds and the chopped chilli
• Cook for 1 minute • Add the chopped beets
and cook for 5 minutes, stirring • Pour the
stock into the pan, cover and leave to simmer
for 1 hour

Make the topping • Tip the pumpkin seeds into
the small frying pan and place over a medium-
high heat • Toast until the seeds start to pop •
Add the remaining tablespoon of cumin seeds
and a glug of olive oil • Take off the heat and
set aside

Finish the soup • Take the saucepan off the
heat and let cool a little • Roughly chop the
dill • Blitz to a smooth soup in the pan or
blender • Taste and season generously with
salt and pepper • Ladle into bowls and top
with a drizzle of dairy-free yoghurt, the
spiced pumpkin seeds, sliced red chilli and
a scattering of fresh dill • Serve with crusty
bread alongside for dipping

WINTER SOUP

Serves 4–6

1 large white onion
600g parsnips
600g carrots
1 tbsp olive oil
handful of fresh coriander
2 garlic cloves
thumb-sized piece of fresh ginger
1 tbsp curry powder
½–1 tsp chilli flakes, plus extra for sprinkling
1 litre vegetable stock
4 tbsp pumpkin seeds
400ml coconut milk, plus extra for drizzling
salt and black pepper

**Large saucepan with a lid over a medium heat •
Small frying pan • Power or stick blender**

Prep the vegetables • Peel and finely chop the
onion • Peel and roughly chop the parsnips •
Roughly chop the carrots • Heat the oil in the
hot saucepan • Add the onion and fry for 5
minutes, stirring occasionally, until softened

Cook the soup • Separate the coriander
leaves and put them to one side • Finely chop
the stems • Peel and roughly chop the garlic
and ginger and add to the pan along with
the coriander stems, curry powder and chilli
flakes • Cook for 1 minute • Add the chopped
vegetables and cook for 5 minutes, stirring
well • Pour the stock into the pan, bring to the
boil, cover and leave to simmer and bubble
for 1 hour

Finish and serve • Meanwhile, tip the pumpkin
seeds into a small frying pan and place over
a high heat to toast • Take the pan off the heat
• Remove the soup pan from the heat and add
the coconut milk • Blend until smooth in the
pan or blender • Taste and season generously
with salt and pepper • Ladle into bowls and
drizzle with more coconut milk • Top with
some chilli flakes, the toasted pumpkin seeds
and the reserved coriander leaves

CARROT & CORIANDER SOUP

Sometimes, the simplest things are the best, and the minimalism in this classic flavour combination is its superpower. This is a BOSH! take on an absolute classic soup flavour combo. To make it that extra bit special, we've loaded the soup with an undercurrent of mellow spice that really complements and elevates the end result. For an extra punch of flavour, try making this with either the Ultimate Veg Stock on page 234.

Serves 8

2 tbsp vegetable oil
1 large or 2 small onions
4 garlic cloves
¾ tsp sweet smoked
    paprika
2 tbsp tomato purée
1.8 litres vegetable stock
    or water
50g fresh coriander
3–4 tsp sherry, cider
    vinegar or ½ lemon
salt and black pepper

For the carrots
2 tbsp vegetable oil
1.5kg carrots
2 tsp coriander seeds
2 tsp cumin seeds
1 tsp black peppercorns
1 tsp fennel seeds
½ tsp chilli flakes
pinch of caraway seeds
    (optional)
1 tbsp maple or golden
    syrup

To serve
extra-virgin olive oil,
    for drizzling
bread, for dipping

Preheat the oven to 180°C · Roasting tin · Large saucepan with a lid · Power or stick blender

Roast the carrots · Pour the oil for the carrots into the roasting tin · Put the tin in the hot oven for 5 minutes · Meanwhile, peel the carrots and cut them into roughly 4cm lengths · Remove the tin from the oven and add the carrots · Roast for 30 minutes · Sprinkle over the spices and syrup and roast for 10 minutes more

Cook the base · Place the saucepan over a medium heat and pour in the oil · Peel and chop the onions and add them to the hot oil · Cover and cook for 8 minutes, until softened and lightly golden · Bash open the garlic and chop the cloves · Turn the heat to low, add the garlic, mix well, cover and cook for 1 minute

Add the carrots · Take the carrots out of the oven and add them to the pot, scraping in all the spices from the base · Add the paprika and tomato purée and mix well · Add the stock or water · Cover, bring to the boil, then reduce the heat to medium and simmer for 10 minutes · Take the pan off the heat · Season and leave to cool to room temperature

Blend the soup · Separate the coriander leaves and stems · Finely chop the stems and roughly chop the leaves · If using a power blender, pour the cooled soup into the blender · Add the coriander stems and the sherry, cider vinegar or squeeze in the lemon juice · Blend until smooth

Serve · When you're ready to serve, warm the soup to simmering in a saucepan over a medium heat · Season to taste with salt and pepper, squeeze in a little lemon juice, if using, and drizzle over a little extra-virgin olive oil · Ladle the soup into bowls, top with the coriander leaves and serve immediately, with bread alongside for dipping

BOMBAY POTATO SALAD

Oh, my goodness, the flavour! This absolute winner of a potato salad is packed with delicious curry spices and topped with crunchy fried onions, fiery sliced chilli and fragrant coriander. Served with mango chutney and cooling raita, it almost deserves main-meal status in its own right! Make a batch and take it to a barbecue – you'll be everyone's best friend, for sure.

Serves 6

600g new potatoes /
    small waxy potatoes
75ml vegetable oil
1 onion
1 tbsp curry powder
1 tsp cumin seeds
1 tsp coriander seeds
1 tsp mustard seeds
handful of fresh
    coriander
½ lemon

For the raita
½ cucumber
4 tbsp dairy-free yoghurt
½ lemon
1 tsp dried mint
salt

To serve
1 fresh red chilli
2 tbsp mango chutney
2 tbsp crispy onions
handful of fresh
    coriander

Medium pan of salted water on a high heat • Large frying pan on a medium heat

Boil the potatoes • Cut any large potatoes into ping-pong-ball-sized pieces, leaving the smaller ones whole • Add to the pan of boiling water and cook for 15 minutes until tender • Drain and leave to steam dry over the hot pan

Fry the onions and potatoes • Pour half of the oil into the hot frying pan • Peel and slice the onion and add it to the pan • Fry for 10 minutes, until starting to colour and crisp • Add the spices, stir for a few minutes to toast, then add the rest of the oil • Turn up the heat and add the potatoes • Season well and toss everything together • Roughly chop the coriander stems and leaves and add them too • Cook until the potatoes and onions are dark brown and crisp • Turn off the heat and squeeze over the lemon juice

Make the raita • Trim the cucumber, cut it in half lengthways and scoop out the watery seeds • Grate into a bowl and season with salt • Add the yoghurt, lemon juice and mint to the bowl and stir everything together to combine

Build the salad • Trim and finely chop the chilli • Pile the potatoes onto a serving plate • Pour over the raita • Spoon over a big dollop of mango chutney • Scatter over the crispy onions and sliced red chilli • Tear over some coriander leaves and serve

GENERAL TSO'S TOFU

This is our plant-based take on the classic Chinese takeaway dish, General Tso's Chicken. It's named after Qing dynasty statesman and military leader, Tso Tsung-t'ang, though no one knows why as it seems unlikely that he ever tasted the dish, which is a shame because it's delicious! Crispy, sticky and sweet, this is tofu at its finest. For an extra nutty flavour, you could toast the sesame seeds briefly in a dry pan before sprinkling over the dish. This goes great with our Home-Made Tofu (page 222).

Serves 2

280g plain firm tofu
3 tbsp tamari soy sauce
1 tbsp apple cider vinegar
4 tbsp cornflour
4 tbsp vegetable oil

For the jasmine rice
150g jasmine rice
300ml cold water
1 jasmine tea bag
    or jasmine flower
1 star anise
1 tsp fine sea salt

For the sauce
4 garlic cloves
2 tbsp cane, coconut
    or brown sugar
1 tbsp cornflour
2 tbsp apple cider vinegar
2 tbsp tamari
    or soy sauce
1 tbsp Chinese vinegar

To serve
1 tbsp sesame seeds
1 tsp dried Szechuan
    chillies or chilli flakes
handful of fresh chives

Non-stick frying pan • Medium saucepan with a lid • Plate lined with kitchen paper

Marinate the tofu • Cut the tofu into 2cm cubes and put it in a bowl with the soy sauce and apple cider vinegar • Toss to coat • Set aside for 10 minutes

Meanwhile, make the jasmine rice • Rinse the rice under cold water for 1 minute • Tip into the saucepan and pour over the water • Add the tea bag or jasmine flower, star anise and salt • Cover and bring to the boil • Turn the heat down to the lowest setting and leave covered for about 12 minutes while you fry the tofu

Fry the tofu • Drain the tofu, setting the marinade aside for the sauce • Put the tofu in a clean bowl with the cornflour and toss to coat • Place the frying pan over a medium-high heat and add the vegetable oil • Fry the cubes in the hot oil until golden brown, then transfer to the plate lined with kitchen paper • Turn off the heat and leave the hot oil in the pan

Make the sauce • Peel and finely slice the garlic and add it to the tofu oil in the pan (it should sizzle and start to go brown) • Measure all the other sauce ingredients into a bowl • Pour in the leftover marinade • Whisk until smooth • Spoon a couple of large spoonfuls of starchy water from the top of the rice pan into the bowl • Turn the heat on to medium and pour in the sauce • Stir until it starts to thicken • Toss in the tofu and stir to coat

Serve • Fluff up the cooked rice with a fork and spoon it into bowls • Top with the tofu • Sprinkle over the sesame seeds and dried Szechuan chillies or chilli flakes, snip over the chives and serve

TINNED TOMATO SOUP
& TINNED TOMATO PASTA

Sometimes your cupboards are bare and all you have left is a tin of tomatoes. Well look no further, friends, we've got you covered. Roasting tinned tomatoes brings out their natural sweetness and imparts a richness that you simply don't get by warming them in a saucepan. If you're a fan of tomatoes you need to give these two recipes a whirl – you'll be blown away by how tasty a tin of tommies can be!

ROASTED TINNED TOMATO SOUP

Serves 2

2 x 400g tins peeled
    plum tomatoes
3 garlic cloves
1 red onion
2 tbsp olive oil
1 tsp sugar
1 tbsp tomato purée
½ tsp dried oregano
500ml vegetable stock
salt and black pepper

For the croûtons
200g crusty bread
2 tbsp olive oil
½ tsp salt
¼ tsp pepper
¼ tsp dried oregano

To serve
olive oil, for drizzling

Preheat the oven to 180°C • Line 1 roasting tin and 1 baking sheet with parchment paper • Place a sieve over a bowl • Power blender

Prepare the ingredients • Pour the tinned tomatoes into the sieve and catch the juice in the bowl • Peel the garlic • Peel and halve the red onion, then cut one half into 4 wedges and dice the other

Roast the tomatoes • Spoon the tomatoes into a roasting tin • Add 2 of the garlic cloves and the onion wedges to the tin • Drizzle over a tablespoon of olive oil, sprinkle over the sugar and season with salt and pepper • Put the tin in the oven and roast for 30 minutes, stirring halfway through

Prepare the croûtons • Cut the bread into 2cm cubes and tip them into a bowl • Add the olive oil, salt, pepper and oregano and toss to combine • Spread the mixture over the lined baking tray, put the tray in the oven and roast for 8–10 minutes, until golden and crispy

Prepare the base • Pour the remaining tablespoon of olive oil into the saucepan and place it over a medium heat • Add the onion and a pinch of salt and cook, stirring, for 4–5 minutes • Crush the remaining garlic clove into the pan and stir for 1 minute • Add the tomato purée and oregano and stir for 2 minutes • Add the reserved tomato juice from the tin and the vegetable stock and simmer for 7–8 minutes • Take the pan off the heat and set aside to cool

Blend the soup • Take the tin out of the oven and leave it to cool for 5–10 minutes • Pour all the ingredients for the soup into the blender and blend until completely smooth • Pour the soup back into the pan and simmer for 5 minutes over a medium heat, then taste and season

Serve • Transfer the soup to serving bowls, top with the crispy croûtons, season with salt and pepper, drizzle with a little olive oil and serve immediately

ROASTED TINNED TOMATO PASTA

Serves 2

400g pasta
12 fresh basil leaves (optional)

For the sauce
2 x 400g tins chopped tomatoes
2 tbsp olive oil
2 tsp sugar, plus extra for seasoning
1 red onion
1 garlic clove
1 tbsp tomato purée
salt and black pepper

Preheat the oven to 200°C • **Line a roasting tin with parchment paper** • **Place a sieve over a bowl** • **Large frying pan I** • **Large saucepan of salted water on a high heat**

Roast the tomatoes • Pour the tomatoes into the sieve and catch the juices in the bowl • Transfer the chopped tomatoes to the lined roasting tin • Drizzle with 1 tablespoon of the olive oil and sprinkle with the 2 teaspoons sugar • Season with salt and pepper • Put the tin in the oven and roast the tomatoes for 30 minutes

Make the base for the sauce • Peel and finely dice the red onion • Pour the remaining olive oil into the frying pan and place over a medium heat • Add the onion to the hot pan with a pinch of salt and stir for 6–7 minutes • Peel the garlic, grate it into the pan and stir for 1 minute • Add the tomato purée and stir

for 1 minute • Add the reserved tomato liquid from the tin, stir and then turn the heat right down to a simmer

Cook the pasta • Add the pasta to the pan of boiling salted water and cook according to packet instructions

Mix and serve • Scrape the roasted tomatoes and all the juices into the frying pan and stir to combine, adding a little pasta water to the pan to loosen it if necessary • Taste and season with salt, pepper and sugar • Drain the pasta and fold it into the sauce • Spoon into bowls, garnish with fresh basil leaves, if using, sprinkle over a little black pepper and serve immediately

HEALTHY DONER KEBAB

This recipe is a homage to one our favourite vegan food spots, What The Pitta in London (Hi Cem!). We love their mezze box so much we decided to make our own! We've made our own vegan meat from scratch a few times but this 'bread meat' is the best yet. The kneading takes a fair bit of elbow grease but, trust us, it's a revelation. Keep going and keep washing (yes, you read that right!) for longer than you think and you'll get a deliciously meaty result. You won't believe how good the texture is, and the herbs give the MOST incredible flavour.

Serves 4

1kg strong white
 bread flour
600ml water
1 tbsp olive oil

For the pickled red
cabbage
120ml red wine vinegar
120ml water
1 tbsp caster sugar
1 tbsp salt
¼ tsp black pepper
¼ red cabbage

For the tzatziki
½ cucumber
1½ tbsp salt
½ lemon
1 small garlic clove
½ tsp dried mint
200g plain plant-based
 yoghurt
salt and black pepper
olive oil, for drizzling

For the couscous
200g couscous
1 tsp salt
½ tsp pepper
1 small red onion
1 red pepper
30g fresh parsley
2 tbsp olive oil

For the marinade
4 tbsp vegetable oil
4 tbsp red wine vinegar
2 tbsp soy sauce
1 tbsp dried oregano
2 tsp dried rosemary
2 tsp dried thyme
1 tsp smoked paprika
1 tsp sugar
salt and black pepper

Sealable container • Clean work surface dusted liberally with flour • 2 clean tea towels • Kettle boiled • Large saucepan with a lid • Heatproof colander • Frying pan • Serving boxes

Make the pickled red cabbage • Add the red wine vinegar, water, sugar, salt and black pepper to a sealable container and stir to combine • Core the red cabbage and shred the red part of the leaves • Add it to the container, put the lid on, shake and leave to pickle for at least 2 hours • Once pickled, drain (reserving the juices for more pickling!) and set aside

Start the bread meat • Measure the flour and water into a bowl and stir to combine • Tip on to the dusted work surface • Work the dough aggressively for at least 10 minutes, ideally 15, really pulling, stretching and folding the dough – it should feel like hard work • Once it's come together into a nice ball, the real work begins • Grip the dough at the bottom of the ball and slap it down on the counter twice with a flicking action that will lengthen and stretch the ball • Press the elongated ball of dough together and repeat this process for 10 minutes – firmness and aggression is the key here • Bring the dough together into a ball, return it to the bowl, cover with a clean tea towel and leave to rest for 1 hour

Meanwhile, make the tzatziki • Peel the cucumber and coarsely grate it into a bowl • Sprinkle over the salt and stir to coat • Set aside for 15 minutes • Tip the cucumber into the middle of a clean tea towel, gather up the edges and squeeze out the excess water • Return the strained cucumber to the bowl • Squeeze over the juice of the lemon, catching any pips in your other hand • Peel the garlic and finely grate it into the bowl • Add the dried mint • Pour over the yoghurt and mix everything together with a spoon • Taste and season to perfection with salt, pepper and a drizzle of olive oil

Make the couscous • Tip the couscous, salt and pepper into a bowl • Pour over boiling water so that the couscous is covered by 5mm of water • Cover and set aside for 5 minutes, until the couscous is nice and fluffy • Peel and finely dice the red onion • Halve, core and dice the pepper • Pick the parsley leaves and finely slice half, reserving

To serve
½ iceberg lettuce
100g hummus
16 pitted black and
     green olives
4 tbsp chilli sauce

the whole leaves for garnish • Fluff the couscous with a fork, add the red onion, red pepper, olive oil and chopped parsley • Fold to combine

Prepare the extras • Halve the lettuce, cut out the core and finely shred the leaves • Set aside

Finish the bread meat • Fill the sink with water • Transfer the ball of dough to the water and wash, rubbing the dough with your hands • Drain the water and run the tap again a good few times until the water runs nearly clear (be patient, it can take about 10 minutes) • Once the water runs almost clear, transfer the dough to a chopping board and press it out with your fingers until it's about 1cm thick (this will be a little tricky as the dough will be quite springy)

Steam the bread meat • Pour water into the saucepan until it's 5cm deep and place it over a high heat • Place the stretched dough into a colander and put the colander on top of the hot pan • Put the lid on top of the colander and steam for 20 minutes, until the raw dough has cooked (if it looks like it needs longer, flip it over and give it another 5–10 minutes • Transfer the dough to a chopping board and leave to cool • Cut into 1½cm strips

Marinate the bread meat • Measure all the marinade ingredients into a shallow bowl and stir to mix • Add the bread meat, stir to coat, cover and leave to marinate in the fridge for 20 minutes

Cook the bread meat • Place the frying pan over a medium heat and add the tablespoon of olive oil • Add the marinated bread meat along with the marinade to the hot oil and stir for 4–5 minutes, until cooked through and beginning to crisp at the edges

Build the kebab boxes • Spoon the couscous, bread meat, pickled red cabbage, tzatziki, shredded lettuce, hummus and olives into the boxes • Drizzle over the chilli sauce, sprinkle over the parsley leaves and serve immediately

SWEET POTATO SALSA SALAD

If you're looking for a tasty, healthy salad that's hearty enough to be eaten as a main, look no further. This salad is deliciously, healthily sweet and fresh tasting. If you want to get ahead, roast the sweet potatoes and make the salsa ahead of time, then just assemble everything when you're ready to serve. If you're off to a barbecue, take this. If you're prepping for a party, make this. If you are a living, breathing human with tastebuds, this is for you!

Serves 4

4 sweet potatoes
    (about 1kg)
4 tbsp olive oil
1 tbsp smoked paprika
3 garlic cloves
250g cherry tomatoes
1 x 200g tin sweetcorn
1 x 400g tin black beans
2 red peppers
75g pumpkin seeds
salt and black pepper

For the salsa
2–3 limes
1 red onion
1 jalapeño
1 large avocado
small bunch of fresh
    coriander
2 tbsp extra-virgin
    olive oil
salt and black pepper

Preheat the oven to 180°C · Large roasting tin · Frying pan

Make the sweet potatoes · Peel the sweet potatoes and cut them into 2cm chunks · Tip them into the roasting tin and drizzle with 2 tablespoons of the olive oil · Season with salt and pepper, sprinkle over the smoked paprika and give everything a good toss · Add the unpeeled garlic cloves · Put the tin in the oven and roast for 30–40 minutes, until the sweet potatoes and garlic are totally soft · Set aside to cool to room temperature

Meanwhile, make the salsa · Zest the limes into a bowl and squeeze the juice over the top · Halve, peel and finely chop the red onion · Stem and finely slice the jalapeño and add it to the bowl · Halve and stone the avocado, dice the flesh and scoop it into the bowl · Finely chop most of the coriander and add it to the salsa, reserving a few leaves for garnish · Drizzle in the extra-virgin olive oil, season well with salt and pepper and toss to combine

Prepare the rest of the salad · Halve the cherry tomatoes · Drain the sweetcorn and black beans and rinse well · Stem and dice the peppers · Place the frying pan over a medium high heat, add the pumpkin seeds and toast until they start to pop · Take the pan off the heat

Assemble and serve · Pop the cooled garlic cloves out of their skins into the salsa and discard the skins · Toss to combine · Tip the tomatoes, sweetcorn, black beans and red peppers into the roasting tin with the sweet potato · Drizzle with the remaining olive oil, season with salt and toss gently to combine · Tip on to a serving plate · Top with the salsa, toasted pumpkin seeds and the reserved coriander leaves and serve

CHEESE & ONION TARTE TATIN

This is the kind of thing you'll want to rustle up if you're hosting a dinner party – your guests will be totally blown away by your culinary prowess. It looks the business, tastes delicious and is a great way to use up any onions you have knocking about in the cupboard. We like to use a quick and easy pastry sheet from the supermarket rather than making our own, but that's your choice, of course. Quick word of advice: you might want to open a bottle for this one . . .

Serves 8 as a starter /
4 as a main

7 mixed red and
    white onions (about
    500–600g)
3 tbsp vegetable oil
1 tbsp dairy-free butter
10 sage leaves
1 tbsp sugar
2–3 tbsp balsamic vinegar
20g smoked
    dairy-free Cheddar
1 x 375g sheet ready-
    rolled dairy-free
    puff pastry
salt and black pepper

To serve
green salad

Preheat the oven to 200°C • **24cm deep ovenproof frying pan with a lid over a medium-low heat** • **Board or plate that will fit tightly over the pan**

Cook the onions • Peel and halve the onions • Add the oil, dairy-free butter and the sage leaves to the hot pan • After a couple of minutes, pour off a little of the sage butter into a small bowl and set the crispy sage leaves aside on a sheet of kitchen paper • Add the onion halves to the pan, cut-sides down • Season generously with salt and pepper, sprinkle the sugar over the onions and drizzle over 1 tablespoon of the balsamic vinegar • Turn down the heat, cover the pan and cook for 15 minutes • Finely grate the Cheddar

Build the tart • Unroll the pastry and cut it in half widthways to make fitting the pastry into the pan easier • Take the lid off the pan and scatter half the cheese over the onions • Drape the two pieces of pastry over the top to cover the onions (they will overlap in the middle) • Carefully tuck the pastry in around the onions, being careful not to burn your fingers on the side of the pan • Prick the pastry all over with a fork and brush the top with the reserved sage butter • Transfer the pan to the hot oven to bake for 25 minutes, until golden brown and puffed up

Serve • Remove the pan from the oven (the handle will be hot!) • Lay the board or plate over the pan then carefully flip it over to tip out the tart • Drizzle over the remaining balsamic vinegar, reserved cheese and the fried sage leaves • Slice and serve with a simple green salad

LOCKDOWN CURRY RAMEN

Time to get your slurp on for this steaming bowl of yummy noodles with loads of veggies and delicious broth. This is one of those dishes that has the ability to make everything immediately seem better; the kind of comfort food we hankered for during the 2020 lockdown, guaranteed to buoy your spirits and fill your belly with warmth, no matter how stressful a day you've had. Plus, this bowl is filled with goodness, so you'll feel virtuous too.

Serves 4

250g mixed mushrooms
200g extra-firm tofu
60g watercress
1 large carrot
3 spring onions
1 fresh red chillies
15g fresh coriander
   or mint leaves
200g noodles (udon
   work great)
1 litre vegetable stock
2 tbsp vegetable oil
salt

For the spicy sauce
2 large garlic cloves
1–2 fresh red chillies
2½ tbsp shichimi
   togarashi spice mix
2 tbsp curry powder
2 tbsp sugar
6 tbsp soy sauce
4 tbsp sesame oil
4 tbsp white wine vinegar

Large saucepan of salted water on a high heat • Small saucepan • Blender • Wok

Prep your veg • Roughly chop the mushrooms into 3cm chunks and the tofu into 1.5cm chunks • Remove any very thick stems from the watercress and roughly chop the leaves and remaining stems • Peel the carrot and cut it into ribbons with a peeler • Trim and finely slice the spring onions and chillies • Trim any rough ends from your herbs and roughly chop the leaves and lighter stems

Cook the noodles • Place your noodles in the boiling salted water and cook according to packet instructions • Drain and rinse under cold water

Make a stock • Place the small saucepan over a medium heat • Add the vegetable stock and bring to a simmer • Measure all the ingredients for the sauce into a blender and blitz • Pour half the sauce into the saucepan with the vegetable stock • Bring to a low simmer and leave to bubble away while you cook your veg

Fry the veg • Place the wok on a high heat and add the vegetable oil • When the oil is hot, add the mushrooms and tofu and fry for 7 minutes, stirring regularly, until the mushrooms and tofu have darkened significantly • Add the remaining sauce and fry for another 2 minutes

Bring it all together • Divide the noodles between serving bowls • Pour over the simmering stock • Top with the stir-fried mushrooms and noodles • Scatter over the watercress, carrot, chilli, spring onions and herbs and serve

STICKY TERIYAKI AUBERGINE

This is a dish that you'd expect to find in a restaurant. The aubergine is perfectly cooked and brimming with magnificently punchy flavours. It's so Instagram worthy, it's ridiculous. Make this for your better half and you'll be sure to earn a fair few aubergine emojis!

Serves 4

1 tbsp vegetable oil
2 large aubergines
(about 650g)
2 tbsp sesame oil

For the rice
200g basmati rice
600ml boiling water
1 tbsp vegetable oil
salt and black pepper

For the carrot salad
4 spring onions
½ fresh red chilli
¼ red cabbage
(about 350g)
2 carrots
4 tbsp sesame seeds

For the salad dressing
2 tbsp light soy sauce
2 tbsp rice wine vinegar
1 tbsp caster sugar
1 tbsp sesame oil
pinch of salt

For the teriyaki sauce
40g dark brown sugar
35g soy sauce
175ml + 1 tbsp water
1 small garlic clove
3cm piece fresh ginger
2 tsp cornflour
½ lime

To serve
180g edamame beans
1 lime

Small saucepan with a lid • Kettle boiled • Line a baking tray • Small saucepan

Cook the rice • Rinse the rice under cold running water and tip it into the saucepan • Put the pan on the hob, add the boiling water and a pinch of salt, cover and bring to the boil over a high heat • Stir once to loosen, then reduce the heat to a very low simmer • Cover and cook for exactly 12 minutes • Take the pan off the heat and set it to one side, leaving the lid on but with a small gap to let out steam

Meanwhile, cook the aubergines • Heat the grill to max • Drizzle a little oil over the aubergines and rub it into the skin • Slice them in half and use a sharp knife to crosshatch the flesh • Place on the lined baking tray, flesh-side up • Drizzle with 1 tablespoon of the sesame oil • Grill for 15 minutes, until blackened and collapsing • Turn and grill for 5 more minutes to soften the skin

Make the carrot salad • Trim and finely slice the spring onions and chilli • Set aside a few for garnish, putting the rest in a bowl • Finely shred the red cabbage • Cut the carrots into matchsticks • Add the cabbage and carrots to the bowl and toss to mix • Sprinkle over about 3 tablespoons of the sesame seeds • Mix together all the dressing ingredients in a small bowl and sprinkle it over the salad • Toss everything together • Taste and season with salt, if needed • Set aside

Make the teriyaki sauce • Measure the brown sugar, soy sauce and 175ml water into a small saucepan • Peel and finely grate the garlic and ginger into the pan • Turn the heat to high and bring to the boil • Mix the cornflour with the 1 tablespoon of water and pour the mixture into the pan • Turn down the heat and whisk for about 5–10 minutes, until you have a thick, glossy sauce • Squeeze in the juice of the lime and set aside

Caramelise the aubergines • Turn the aubergines again so that they're flesh-side up • Spoon half the teriyaki sauce over the top and slide them back under the grill for 5–10 minutes more, until sticky and charred

Serve • Toss the rice with the tablespoon of oil, season well and divide among the bowls • Top each with a big spoonful of carrot salad, a tablespoon of edamame beans and an aubergine half • Drizzle with extra teriyaki sauce and top with the reserved sesame seeds, spring onions and chilli • Slice the remaining lime into wedges and serve on the side

BLACK BEAN SOUP & CHILLI CORNBREAD

This delicious, hearty soup is packed with protein-rich black beans, sweet kernels of corn and rich in warming Tex-Mex flavours. Served with a beautifully tender, crumbly cornbread that's laced with just a hint of spice and perfect for dipping, this is a magnificent meal that will leave you and your guests with satisfied stomachs and contented ear-to-ear grins.

Serves 4

3 spring onions
5 coriander stems
1 tbsp vegetable oil
2 tsp ground coriander
2 tsp ground cumin
2 tsp smoked paprika
½ tsp chilli flakes
1 x 400g tin black beans
  in water
80g frozen sweetcorn
1 x 400g tin chopped
  tomatoes
½ vegetable stock cube
450ml water
salt

For the cornbread
150g plain flour
100g cornflour or polenta
2 tsp baking powder
1 tsp salt
200ml dairy-free milk
1 tbsp vegetable oil
1 tbsp maple syrup
140g frozen sweetcorn
1 tbsp chipotle
  chilli flakes
1½ tbsp dairy-free butter,
  for greasing

To serve
4 tbsp dairy-free
  yoghurt
½ lime

Preheat the oven to 200°C · 20–23cm skillet or heavy-based ovenproof frying pan · Cooling rack · Large saucepan

Make the cornbread dough · Measure the dry ingredients into a bowl and mix to combine · Measure the milk, vegetable oil and maple syrup into a separate bowl · Add the sweetcorn and chipotle flakes · Pour the wet mixture into the dry ingredients and stir everything together to form a dough

Cook the cornbread · Place the skillet or frying pan over a medium heat · Melt the dairy-free butter in the hot pan, moving it around to coat the sides · When the butter starts to bubble, pour in the batter · Transfer the pan to the hot oven for 25 minutes · Take the pan out of the oven (the handle will be hot!) · Carefully remove the cornbread and leave it to cool on a rack

Meanwhile, make the soup · Trim and finely chop the spring onions · Put the chopped green tops to one side · Pick the coriander leaves and finely chop the stems · Place the saucepan over a medium heat · Pour in the oil · Add the white spring onion and coriander stems and cook for a few minutes · When they are starting to soften, add the spices and stir for 1 minute · Add the black beans with their water, the sweetcorn, chopped tomatoes, stock cube and water · Taste and season · Bring to a gentle simmer and cook for 10–15 minutes, until thickened

Serve · Pour the soup into bowls and garnish with the green spring onion tops, a spoonful of dairy-free yoghurt , the coriander leaves and a squeeze of lime

VIETNAMESE-STYLE NOODLE SALAD

This salad is proof that healthy food can be outrageously delicious. The flavours are punchy, zingy and zesty and the textures are brilliantly crunchy and crispy. It's a party in your mouth. It helps to have a ribbon peeler to prepare the veg for this, but you can pick one up very cheaply. If you can't get hold of one, a sharp knife and little patience will do the same job.

Serves 4

280g firm tofu
2 medium carrots
1 cucumber
4 spring onions
1 romaine lettuce
30g fresh coriander
10g fresh mint
1 fresh red chilli
200g rice vermicelli
    noodles
salt
vegetable oil, for frying

For the dressing
5cm piece fresh ginger
1 garlic clove
2 tbsp caster sugar
1 tsp dried chilli flakes
4 tbsp light soy sauce
4 tbsp rice vinegar
2 tbsp rapeseed oil

To serve
1 lime
25g salted peanuts

Tofu press or 2 clean tea towels and a weight • Large frying pan • Line a plate with kitchen paper • Small frying pan • Kettle boiled

Cook the tofu • Press the tofu for at least 10 minutes using the tofu press or for at least 30 minutes placed between two clean tea towels with a heavy weight on top • Place the pressed tofu on its side and cut it lengthways into 4 sheets • Pour oil into the large frying pan until it's 1cm deep and place over a medium heat • Lay the tofu sheets in the hot oil and fry on both sides until golden brown and crispy • Transfer to the plate lined with kitchen paper to drain • Cut the tofu sheets into matchsticks • Season with a little salt and set aside

Prepare the vegetables and herbs • Peel, trim and shred the carrots into matchsticks • Cut the cucumber in half lengthways, scoop out the watery seeds and cut into matchsticks • Trim the spring onions, cut them into 5-cm lengths and finely slice • Cut the lettuce lengthways into quarters and cut out the white centres • Shred the leaves • Pick the herb leaves, discard the mint stems and finely slice the coriander stems • Trim and finely slice the chilli • Cut the lime into wedges

Prepare the peanuts • Put the peanuts in a dry pan and fry over a medium heat until golden

Cook the noodles • Place the noodles in a bowl, cover with boiling water and leave to soak for 8 minutes • Drain and return to the mixing bowl • Cover with cold water and leave to soak for 1 minute • Drain

Make the dressing • Peel and finely grate the ginger and garlic • Add to a small bowl along with the rest of the dressing ingredients • Stir to combine

Build the salad • Put the carrot, cucumber, spring onion, lettuce, half the coriander, half the mint and three quarters of the dressing into a bowl and toss to coat • Divide between serving bowls • Sprinkle over the remaining herbs, the chopped red chilli and toasted peanuts • Drizzle over the remaining dressing • Top with the tofu matchsticks and serve immediately with lime wedges

WINTER WALDORF SALAD

Who says salad is only for the warmer months? Done right, salads can be comforting, hearty and great even in cold weather. With this recipe we've taken the classic Waldorf flavours of apples, grapes and walnuts and added generous wedges of roasted celeriac and protein- and fibre-rich butter beans for added goodness and comfort.

Serves 4

For the celeriac
1 small celeriac (1kg
    unpeeled,
    550g peeled)
2 tbsp olive oil
salt and black pepper

For the salad
100g walnuts
1 x 400g tin butter beans
2 apples (we used
    Braeburn)
100g seedless red grapes
4 celery sticks
1 small iceberg lettuce

For the dressing
8 tbsp plant-based mayo
1 lemon
salt and black pepper

To serve
fresh chives

Preheat the oven to 180°C • 2 roasting tins

Prepare the celeriac • Peel the celeriac with a small sharp knife and cut it into 8 wedges • Put in a roasting tin, drizzle with the olive oil and season • Put the tin in the oven and roast for 45 minutes

Meanwhile, prepare the salad • Put the walnuts in the other roasting tin, put the tin in the oven and roast for 6–8 minutes, or until golden • Rinse the butter beans under cold water • Core, halve and finely slice the apples • Halve the grapes • Trim and finely slice the celery • Trim and shred the lettuce

Make the dressing • Put the plant-based mayo into a bowl • Halve the lemon and squeeze in the juice • Season with salt and pepper and stir to combine

Finish the salad • Add the walnuts, butter beans, apples, grapes and celery to the dressing bowl and toss to coat

Build the bowls • Spread the shredded lettuce over the bottom of your serving bowls • Top with the crunchy walnut and apple mixture • Take the celeriac out of the oven and top each salad with 2 wedges • Garnish with snipped chives and serve immediately

LEMON TOFU

This fresh and zesty take on the Americanised Chinese takeaway classic is full of bright, citrusy flavour. It's sweet, sour, tangy and tasty, perfect on its own or in a Chinese-style spread. As long as your tofu is pressed, it can be on the table in the time that it takes to cook your rice, so it's a great midweek option for when you want something light and flavourful in a hurry.

Serves 2

280g firm tofu
40g cornflour
40g flour
250ml vegetable oil,
    for deep-frying

For the marinade
1 garlic clove
5cm piece fresh ginger
2 tbsp soy sauce
1 tbsp water
pinch of chilli flakes

For the lemon sauce
45ml water
1 tbsp cornflour
45g agave or maple syrup
1 lemon

For the rice
150g basmati rice
500ml boiling water
salt

To serve
2 spring onions
1 tbsp sesame seeds
½ lemon

Tofu press or 2 clean tea towels and a weight • Small saucepan • Small saucepan with a lid • Wok • Line a large plate with kitchen paper

Prepare the ingredients • Press the tofu for at least 10 minutes using the tofu press or place it between two clean tea towels, lay it on a plate and put a weight on top • Peel and grate the garlic and ginger • Zest the lemon for the sauce and cut it in half • Slice the spring onions

Marinate the tofu • Put the soy sauce, water, garlic, ginger and chilli flakes into a bowl and stir to combine • Take the tofu out of the press and rip it into strips no more than 1cm thick • Put them in the bowl and stir to coat them in the marinade • Cover and set aside

Make the lemon sauce • Put the 45ml of water and tablespoon of cornflour into a small bowl and mix to make a slurry • Put the small pan over a medium heat • Add the syrup, lemon zest and juice and bring to a gentle simmer • Add the cornflour slurry and stir to combine • Turn the heat right down

Cook the rice • Rinse the rice under cold running water and tip it into the saucepan • Put the pan on the hob, add the boiling water and a pinch of salt, cover and bring to the boil over a high heat • Stir once to loosen, then reduce the heat to a very low simmer • Cover and cook for exactly 12 minutes • Take the pan off the heat and set it to one side, leaving the lid on but with a small gap to let out steam

Cook the tofu • Place the wok on a high heat and add the oil • Heat to 180°C, or until the oil sizzles around the edges when you dip in a wooden spoon • Add the cornflour and flour to a bowl and stir to combine • Transfer the marinated tofu to the bowl and toss it in the flour to coat • Deep-fry the tofu in batches until the strips are crispy and golden • Transfer to the lined plate

Finish the lemon tofu and serve • Toss the crispy tofu pieces in the sticky lemon sauce, adding a splash more water if needed to loosen it • Spoon the rice into bowls then lay the tofu pieces over the top • Slice the remaining lemon half and place a wedge on each bowl • Garnish with the sliced spring onions and the sesame seeds and serve immediately

FOOD FOR FRIENDS

BANGIN' BAO BUNS

Bao buns are SO GOOD! Little fluffy pillows of edible heaven stuffed with all that is sticky, spicy and sweet. They're basically the perfect food. We've given you three filling options here: a sticky glazed aubergine, a sweet and saucy shiitake mushroom and a fiery jackfruit bulgogi. Each filling option makes enough for eight to ten bao buns, so pick one filling per batch of buns, or triple up the bun recipe and make all three fillings for a brilliant bao bun banquet! Do follow the recipe carefully, as bao buns can be temperamental little things and, of course, you can buy the buns if you prefer!

Makes 8-10

500g plain flour, plus
    extra for dusting
½ tsp fine salt
1 x 7g sachet fast-action
    dried yeast
30g caster sugar
15g baking powder
50g unsweetened
    soy milk
250g warm water
25g vegetable oil

Kettle boiled · Saucepan with a lid or a steamer pan · Small saucepan · Oven preheated to 25°C · Wok · Kettle boiled · Clean damp cloth · Line a 2-tier bamboo steamer with parchment paper and puncture it with scissors or the end of a chopstick

Mix the dry ingredients · Measure the flour, salt, yeast, sugar and baking powder into a bowl and stir to combine

Add the wet ingredients · Pour the soy milk and warm water into a jug and stir to combine · Pour one-fifth of the mixture into the bowl and fold it into the dry ingredients · Repeat until the mixture starts to come together into big, dry clumpy shreds with a moist but not too sticky consistency (you may need a little more liquid) · Use your fingers to scoop and your palms to press until the dough comes together

Knead the dough · Turn the dough out onto a clean work surface and knead for 2 minutes to activate the gluten in the flour, pulling, punching and slapping the dough to bring it together and give it elasticity · When it's begun to come together but is still a little grainy, pour over the oil and continue to knead for a further 8 minutes to get a smooth dough. Add a little more flour if the dough is too sticky

Let it rest · When you have a nice smooth ball, dust the dough with a little flour · Lightly oil the bowl, put the dough back in and lightly brush the top with more oil · Cover with a damp cloth, put the bowl in the warm oven and leave it to rest and rise for 60-90 minutes

Shape the buns · Divide the dough into 8 equal pieces and use your hands to shape them into neat little balls · Lightly flour a clean work surface and roll one ball into a 10cm disk, leaving a little lip of dough at each end · Brush the dough with a little oil, lay a chopstick across the middle and gently fold it over · Pull out the chopstick, set the bun to one side and repeat until you have 8 buns ready to steam

Steam the buns · Put the wok over medium heat · Pour in enough hot water to come 3cm up the sides of the pan · Load up the steamer with 4 buns per tier, making sure the bao have enough room to rise · Put the steamer on the wok, put the lid on and steam the buns for 8–10 minutes · Remove the steamer, uncover and leave the buns to rest for 1 minute · Transfer to a plate and they're ready to serve

AUBERGINE GUA BAO

Makes 8

1 large aubergine

For the marinade
1 garlic clove
½ tbsp granulated white sugar
½ tsp five spice powder
½ tsp salt
¼ tsp white pepper
2 tbsp maltose or maple syrup
1 tbsp hot water
½ tbsp hoisin sauce
½ tbsp shaoxing rice wine
½ tbsp soy sauce
½ tsp sesame oil

To serve
2 tbsp roasted peanuts
1 fresh red chilli
½ cucumber
8 bao buns

Preheat the oven to 180°C • Baking tray lined with tin foil • Microwavable bowl • Line a plate with kitchen paper

Prepare the aubergine • Prick the aubergine all over with a fork and put it in the microwavable bowl • Microwave for 10 minutes • Transfer to the plate lined with kitchen paper and leave to cool • Once cool, remove the top, peel off the skin and cut in half lengthways

Marinade the aubergine • Peel and mince the garlic • Measure all the marinade ingredients into a bowl and stir to combine • Place the aubergine in the marinade and leave to marinate for 10–15 minutes

Prepare the remaining ingredients • Crush the peanuts • Trim and finely slice the red chilli • Trim the cucumber, cut it in half lengthways, scoop out the watery seeds with a spoon and finely slice • Transfer the ingredients to serving bowls

Roast the aubergine • Lift the aubergine on to the baking tray • Put it in the hot oven and roast for 5 minutes • Turn the aubergine, glaze it with the remaining marinade, return it to the oven and roast for another 7–10 minutes, until most of the marinade has become a nice sticky glaze

Serve • Slice the aubergine and transfer it to a serving bowl • Set the bao buns, aubergine, peanuts, chilli and cucumber on the table, fill your bao buns and tuck in!

HOISIN MUSHROOM

Makes 8

120g shiitake mushrooms
70ml mirin
70ml sake
70ml light soy sauce

To serve
½ cucumber
4 spring onions
70ml hoisin sauce
8 bao buns

Small saucepan over a medium heat

Marinate the mushrooms • Stem and finely slice the mushrooms • Shred the stems and add them to a bowl with the rest of the mushroom slices • Measure the mirin, sake and soy sauce into the saucepan and bring to a simmer • Once the sauce is bubbling, add the mushrooms and cook until the sauce is reduced and the mushrooms are glazed

Prepare the remaining ingredients • Peel, trim and finely slice the cucumber • Peel, trim and finely slice the spring onions

Serve • Transfer the cucumber, spring onions, hoisin sauce, mushrooms and bao buns to serving bowls, bring them to the table, fill your bao buns and tuck in!

JACKFRUIT BULGOGI

Makes 8

200g tinned jackfruit in water
½ pear
1 garlic clove
½ tbsp ginger
1 tbsp soy sauce
1 tbsp light brown sugar
1 tbsp toasted sesame oil
½ tbsp gochujang paste
1 tbsp vegetable oil
salt and black pepper

For the pickled cucumber
½ cucumber
1 tsp salt
1 tbsp sugar

To serve
2 spring onions
1 carrot
1 tbsp toasted sesame seeds
kimchi (optional, see page 173)
8 bao buns

Medium heavy-based frying pan

Prepare the filling • Drain the jackfruit and crush it between your fingers until it resembles pulled pork • Peel, core and coarsely grate the pear • Peel and finely grate the garlic and ginger • Add the soy sauce, sugar, sesame oil, garlic, ginger and gochujang to a bowl and stir to combine • Add the jackfruit and pear and fold it into the marinade

Pickle the cucumber • Peel and finely slice the cucumber • Cover with a teaspoon of salt and a tablespoon of sugar • Gently toss to coat and leave to marinate for 10 minutes • Drain off the liquid

Prepare the remaining ingredients • Trim, peel and finely slice the spring onion • Trim, peel and slice the carrot into ribbons

Cook the jackfruit • Place the pan over a high heat and add the oil • Add the marinated jackfruit to the hot pan and stir for 5 minutes • Reduce the heat to low and cook for 4 minutes, stirring occasionally • Taste and season with salt and pepper

Time to serve • Transfer the jackfruit, bao buns, sesame seeds, carrots, cucumber and kimchi, if using, to serving bowls • Take the bowls over to the table, fill your bao buns and tuck in!

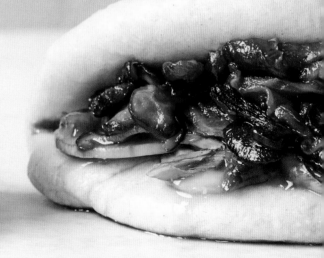

TEMPURA CRUDITÉS

We felt it was high time that someone took crudités and made them waaaaay better. We've BOSHified them by deep-frying them in super crispy tempura batter and serving them with a trio of tasty dips to transform crudités from boring to brilliant! These are fantastic served as a sharer with drinks at a party or even as a starter at a sit-down dinner. And these dipping sauces are great with any Asian side or salad.

Serves 4

125g baby sweetcorn
75g sugar snap peas
125g carrot
75g red pepper
sea salt flakes
vegetable oil, for
    deep frying

For the batter
140g plain flour
2 tbsp cornflour
1 tbsp baking powder
1 tsp salt
250ml chilled
    sparking water

Make your dressing of choice (see below) • Wok • Line a tray with kitchen paper

Prepare the batter • Sieve the flour, cornflour, baking powder and salt into a bowl and stir to combine • Gradually pour in the sparkling water, whisking constantly until you have a smooth batter with the consistency of thick custard (add more flour if needed)

Prepare the vegetables • Halve the baby sweetcorn lengthways • Trim the sugar snaps • Peel the carrot and cut it into batons • Trim the pepper and cut it into 1cm thick slices

Fry the tempura crudités • Pour the oil into the wok until it's 5–8cm deep • Heat to 180°C, or until the oil sizzles around the edges when you dip in a wooden spoon • Dip the sweetcorn to coat them in the batter and use tongs to gently transfer them to the oil • Use a teaspoon to drip a little more batter over the baby corn (this will help make them even crispier) • Fry for 3–4 minutes until crunchy and golden, turning halfway • Transfer to the lined tray and repeat to cook all the vegetables

Serve • Transfer the tempura to a serving plate, sprinkle with a little salt and serve immediately with the dipping sauces

DIPPING SAUCES

SRIRACHA MAYO

2 tbsp plant-based mayo
2 tsp rice vinegar
2 tsp sriracha
½ tsp salt

Measure all the ingredients into a small bowl • Mix well and serve

SOY & MAPLE

2.5cm piece fresh ginger
1 small fresh red chilli
2 tbsp soy sauce
1 tbsp maple syrup
    or sugar
1 tbsp rice vinegar
1 tsp sesame oil

Peel and grate the ginger • Trim and finely slice the chilli • Add the ginger, chilli and all the remaining ingredients to a bowl • Mix and serve

HOISIN & ORANGE

½ orange
2 tbsp hoisin sauce
1 tsp rice vinegar

Squeeze the orange juice into a small bowl, catching any pips in your spare hand • Add the hoisin sauce and vinegar • Mix and serve

VEG PAKORAS & MIXED CHUTNEYS

We're firm believers that any curry can be taken to the next level when served with a delicious side of crunchy pakora. We played around with a bunch of different recipes before landing on these two absolute winners. The Saag Aloo brings together the classic combo of potatoes and spinach and is great in summer, while the Carrot & Parsnip has a lovely earthy sweetness and is perfect for the winter months. Both work incredibly well with the inventively delicious chutneys. Enjoy!

Makes 10 pakoras

1 x flavour combination of your choice (see below)

For the batter
200g gram flour
2 tsp salt
1 tsp cumin
1 tsp curry powder
1 tsp ground turmeric
½ tsp bicarbonate of soda
½ tsp garlic powder
½ tsp onion powder
180ml warm water
½ tbsp cider vinegar
vegetable oil, for deep frying

Deep-sided frying pan • Cooking thermometer (optional) • Line a plate with kitchen paper • Metal tablespoon (not a measuring spoon) • Metal slotted spoon

Prepare the batter • Measure all the batter ingredients into a bowl and whisk to a smooth, quite thick batter

Prepare the ingredients • Prepare your chosen vegetables, herbs and spices (below) • Add them to the batter and stir to combine

Time to fry • Pour the vegetable oil into the frying pan until it's 4cm deep • Put the pan over a medium heat and heat to 180°C, or until the oil sizzles around the edges when you dip in a wooden spoon • Use a tablespoon to spoon 4 portions of the batter into the oil keeping some knobbly, gnarly bits to ensure you get a lovely crunchy texture • Use the slotted spoon to gently turn and move the pakoras around in the oil to achieve an even dark-caramel colour • Transfer the pakoras to the lined plate to drain any excess grease • Repeat to use up all the batter • Leave the pakoras to rest and cool down for a couple of minutes before serving

SAAG ALOO PAKORAS

250g potatoes
50g fresh spinach
20g fresh coriander

Prepare the ingredients • Coarsely grate the potatoes • Shred the spinach • Finely chop the coriander • Add the potato, spinach and coriander to the batter and stir to combine • Cook as above

CARROT & PARSNIP PAKORAS

150g carrots
150g parsnips
10g fresh coriander
20g fresh ginger

Prepare the ingredients • Peel, trim and coarsely grate the carrots and parsnips • Finely grate the ginger • Finely chop the coriander • Add the carrot, parsnip, ginger and coriander to the bowl of batter and stir to combine • Cook as above

SULTANA TAMARIND CHUTNEY

Makes enough for 10 pakoras

1 onion
3cm piece fresh ginger
½ tbsp veg oil
½ tsp ground cumin
½ tsp fenugreek seeds
½ tsp ground turmeric
½ tsp mustard seeds
½ tsp salt
¼ tsp chilli flakes
100ml stout (such as Guinness) or water
25ml water
25g sultanas
50ml vinegar
1½ tbsp caster sugar
½ tbsp tamarind paste
¼ orange

Saucepan with a lid over a high heat • Food processor or power blender

Make the chutney • Peel and finely slice the onion • Peel and grate the ginger • Warm the oil in the hot saucepan • Add the onions, spices and salt, stir, cover and sweat the onions for 10 minutes, stirring occasionally, until they start to colour • Add the ginger, stout, water, sultanas, vinegar, sugar and tamarind paste • Stir everything together and simmer over a medium heat with the lid off for 5 minutes, until thickened slightly • Remove a quarter of the mixture and set it to one side in a small bowl • Squeeze the juice from the orange into the pan, stir and allow the chutney to cool to room temperature • Transfer to a food processor and blend until smooth • Pour the blended mixture back into the saucepan and stir over a medium heat for 3–4 minutes • Add the reserved mixture to the pan, stir to combine, then leave to cool to room temperature

CORIANDER CHILLI CHUTNEY

Makes enough for 10 pakoras

4cm piece fresh ginger
1 fresh green chilli
30g fresh coriander
1 lemon
1 tsp garam marsala
1 tsp salt

Power blender

Make the chutney • Peel and roughly chop the ginger • Remove the stem from the chilli • Finely chop the leaves and stems of the coriander • Zest the lemon, cut the lemon in half and squeeze the juice into the blender • Add all the remaining ingredients, including the lemon zest, to the blender and blend until smooth, adding a splash of water to loosen the mixture if necessary

SHIRO WAT & ONE-DAY INJERA

We first tried this classic Ethiopian dish at Habesha Village restaurant in Brixton. It was so good that we simply had to make our own. The Shiro Wat is smooth and fragrant and the injera has a wonderful fluffy texture and delightful sour flavour that develops over a day of resting. Traditionally you'd let the bread rest for longer, but one day is good enough for us! Ethiopian food is traditionally very veggie-friendly, which is one of the reasons we love it so much.

Serves 4

2 white onions
2 tbsp vegetable oil
1 tbsp Berbere Spice Mix
    (see page 120), plus
    a little extra for
    sprinkling
2 garlic cloves
1 tbsp tomato purée
80g gram flour
400ml vegetable stock
40g dairy-free butter
salt

To serve
jalapeños

Prep your injera at least a day ahead (see over the page) • **Small food processor or power blender** • **Large frying pan**

Cook your injera and make your spice mix • Follow the methods over the page to get your injera and spice mix ready

Make the shiro wat • Peel and roughly chop the onions and put them in the food processor or blender • Add the oil and blend to a purée • Put the large frying pan over a medium heat • Add the onion purée • Fry for 12–15 minutes, stirring now and then, until the raw onion smell has gone, the mix is turning brown and the onions are well cooked down • Add the berbere spice mix and stir for a few minutes • Grate in the garlic and stir • Add the tomato purée and cook for another 5 minutes • Sieve the gram flour into the pan and stir for 1 minute to combine • Now slowly add the stock, whisking as you do to make a smooth curry sauce • Simmer for another 5 minutes • Add the butter and stir it in, so that an oily sheen forms on top of the curry • Taste and season

Serve • Lay an injera on each plate and spoon the shiro wat on top • Sprinkle with some jalapeños and a little berbere spice • Tear off pieces of bread at the table and scoop up the curry bit by bit

ONE-DAY INJERA

If you prepare the injera 3–5 days ahead, you can leave out the dried yeast and just let the batter ferment naturally. The longer you leave it to ferment, the more sour and bubbly the bread will be. Don't worry if your first one doesn't quite work – it takes a few tries to get it right!

Makes about 8 Injera

500ml lukewarm water
250g buckwheat flour
¼ tsp dried yeast
¼ tsp baking powder
½ tsp fine salt
2–3 tablespoons oil, for frying

Prep the injera at least a day ahead • Boil the water and let it cool until it's warm • Clean tea towel • Crêpe pan or a 20cm shallow frying pan

The day before, make the dough • Measure the buckwheat flour into a bowl • In a separate bowl, mix the dried yeast with a little of the warm water • Stir the yeast mixture into the flour along with the rest of the water • Cover with a tea towel and leave in a warm place for at least 24 hours until bubbly and smelling nicely sour

Cook the injera • Add the baking powder and salt to the bread dough and mix well • Place the pan over a high heat • Add a little oil and swirl it to coat the pan • When the oil is hot, pour in a ladleful of batter so that it evenly covers the bottom and is just a little thicker than a crêpe would be (little bubbles should appear on the surface) • Lower the heat to medium and cover the pan with a lid, upturned bowl or wok and steam the injera for 2–3 minutes, until browned, slightly crisp on the bottom and cooked through but soft on top with the bubbles still visible • Transfer to a tea towel to keep warm • Increase the heat to high and warm a little more oil, then repeat to make the rest of the injera

BERBERE SPICE MIX

This fiery blend of spices is a staple of Ethiopian and Eritrean cooking. This recipe makes more than you need for the shiro wat recipe, but will keep in a sealed jar for a few months and is also used in our Berbere BBQ Sauce (page 145). If you're making this spice mix before you cook your shiro wat, there's no need to clean the pan as the aromatic pan will add even more flavour to the curry.

Makes 1 small jar

4 cardamom pods
4 dried red chillies
4 whole cloves
4 tsp paprika
2 tsp coriander seeds
1½ tsp salt
1 tsp black peppercorns
1 tsp cumin seeds
1 tsp fenugreek seeds
1 tsp ground allspice
1 tsp ground ginger
1 tsp ground or ½ whole nutmeg
1 tsp ground turmeric
½ tsp ground cinnamon

Frying pan • Spice grinder or pestle and mortar • Clean, sterilised jar

Prepare the spices • Bash the cardamom pods to split them

Make the spice mix • Place the frying pan over a medium heat • Scrape in the cardamom seeds and add the rest of the ingredients, grating in the nutmeg if you're using the whole spice • Lightly toast the spices for a couple of minutes (until your kitchen smells epic!) • Tip the mixture into a spice grinder or pestle and mortar and whizz or grind to a fine powder • Store in a clean, sterilised jar

CRISPY PERSIAN FRIED RICE

We're completely convinced that, when it comes to rice, the crispy bit is always the best bit, and this dish has crispiness in abundance. Traditionally called Tahdig, this Persian dish is a wonderful way of cooking rice that transforms it from something you would serve on the side to very much the star of the meal – a real showstopping party piece! Adding yoghurt to the pan is an incredible hack and pretty much guarantees you a perfectly crisp crown. Deeeelicious!

Serves 4–6

400g basmati rice
100g dairy-free yoghurt
3 tbsp cooking oil
¼ tsp ground turmeric
salt

For the roasted
chickpeas & carrots
500g carrots
2 large onions
1 lemon
3 tbsp olive oil
2 garlic cloves
1 x 400g tin chickpeas
1 tsp ground turmeric
40g raisins or sultanas
salt and black pepper

For the chunky
walnut sauce
60g fresh coriander
30g fresh parsley
4 tbsp extra-virgin
   olive oil
50g raisins or sultanas
100g walnuts
salt and black pepper

To serve
40g raisins or sultanas
handful of pistachios
   (optional)

Preheat the oven to 180°C · Large roasting tin · Medium saucepan · Heavy-based non-stick frying pan or shallow casserole with a lid · Clean tea towel · Power or stick blender

Roast the carrots · Peel and halve the carrots lengthways and cut into 1.5cm thick strips · Peel, halve and slice the onions · Zest the lemon into a small bowl · Halve it and squeeze the juice into a glass · Peel away the flesh and roughly chop it, discarding the skin · Add the onions, carrots and chopped lemon to the roasting tin, drizzle over 2 tablespoons of the oil and toss to coat · Put the tin the oven and roast for 30 minutes

Add the chickpeas · Peel and grate the garlic · Drain, rinse and pat dry the chickpeas · Add the remaining tablespoon of oil, the turmeric and garlic to a bowl and stir to combine · Add the chickpeas and raisins or sultanas, stir to coat and cover · When the carrots have been roasting for 30 minutes, take the tin out of the oven, add the spicy chickpeas and stir to mix · Put the tin back in the oven and roast for a further 10 minutes

Meanwhile, start the rice · Put the rice in a bowl, cover with cold water and leave to soak for 15 minutes · Boil the kettle · Drain the rice and rinse under cold running water for 30 seconds · Add it to the saucepan with a pinch of salt · Put the pan on the hob and pour in enough boiling water so that the rice is covered by 2cm of water · Turn up the heat to a rolling boil and cook for 5 minutes · Drain, rinse with cold water and set aside

Make the crispy base · Add the yoghurt, 2 tablespoons of the oil, the turmeric and a pinch of salt to a bowl and stir to combine · Add just over a third of the rice and stir to coat · Pour a tablespoon of oil into the heavy-based pan and roll it around to cover the base · Add the yoghurty rice and smooth it over the base · Put the pan on the hob, turn the heat to medium and leave for 3–4 minutes · Take the pan off the heat · Meanwhile, lay out the clean tea towel and place the pan lid on top, bring up the corners and tie them around the handle securely

Steam the rice and veg • Spoon the roasted vegetables into the middle of the tin and smooth them into a mound • Season with salt and pepper • Spoon the remaining rice over the top and smooth it out so that the filling is completely covered but the rice doesn't come above the rim of the pan • Press the rice down to compress it • Use a skewer or chop stick to poke a few holes into the rice to let steam escape • Put the prepared lid on the pan and place it over a very low heat • Steam for 50 minutes • Take off the heat and leave to rest for 5 minutes with the lid on

Make the chunky walnut sauce • Pick half the coriander leaves and half the parsley leaves and set them aside • Roughly chop the rest and put them in a food processor along with the olive oil and the reserved lemon juice and zest • Blitz until smooth • Add the raisins or sultanas and walnuts and pulse until roughly combined • Taste and season with salt and pepper

Serve • Take the lid off the rice • Place a large platter over the pan and carefully flip the pan over so that the rice falls on to it • Sprinkle over the reserved herbs, the pistachios, if using, and more raisins or sultanas • Spoon on to serving plates and serve immediately with the walnut sauce on the side

TACOS ACORAZADOS

In Spanish, Acorazados literally means armoured, and the key to success with these delicious bite-sized Mexican tacos is to double wrap the tortilla around the filling to stop it from getting soggy and to keep the filling intact. They are rumoured to have been the favourite snacks of soldiers as the double-wrap meant they were easier to eat on the move! The chorizo recipe here is a revelation: smoky, chewy and just the right amount of spicy. You're in for a treat.

Serves 4–6

For the tomato rice
½ red pepper
1 tbsp vegetable oil
150g long-grain white rice
250ml water
generous pinch of salt
1 tbsp tomato purée

For the chorizo
½ red onion
½ red pepper
1 x 400g tin kidney beans
100g plain flour
50g stale bread
30g sultanas
2 tsp smoked paprika
1 tsp garlic powder
1 tsp ground cinnamon
1 tsp ground coriander
1 tsp ground cumin
2 tsp soy sauce
handful of fresh
    coriander
salt and black pepper
2 tbsp vegetable oil

For the green beans
120g green beans
1–2 tbsp wine or beer
salt

**For the tomato
& apple salsa**
3 large ripe tomatoes
1 apple
½ red onion
pinch of salt
pinch of dried chilli flakes
dash apple cider vinegar
½ lime
handful of fresh
    coriander leaves

To serve
½ lime
16 small soft corn tortillas

Medium saucepan with a lid on a medium heat • **2 clean tea towels** • **Food processor** • **Frying pan with a lid** • **Small saucepan with a lid**

Make the tomato rice • Trim and finely dice the red pepper • Heat the oil in the saucepan and add half of the diced pepper • Stir and turn the heat down to low • Rinse the rice until the water runs clear, then add it to the pan with the water, salt and tomato purée • Stir to combine • Increase the heat, cover and bring to the boil • Once the water is boiling, reduce the heat again and cook on low for another 10 minutes • Take off the heat and cover with a clean tea towel • Just before serving, uncover and fluff up the rice with a fork

Make the chorizo • Peel and roughly chop the onion • Roughly chop the pepper • Drain and rinse the kidney beans • Add all the chorizo ingredients except the vegetable oil to the food processor with a pinch of salt and pepper • Blitz to a thick, chunky paste • Pour half the oil into the frying pan and set it over a medium heat • Spoon in all the chorizo mixture and fry for 10 minutes, allowing a crust to form • Break up the chorizo with a spoon and turn it around in the pan so that you get lots of bite-sized crispy bits • Add the remaining tablespoon of oil and cook for another 5 minutes until crispy • Take the pan off the heat

Cook the green beans • Trim the beans and cut them into 2½cm chunks • Put them in the small pan and add the wine or beer, and a pinch of salt • Cover and cook for 3–5 minutes until tender • Take off the heat

Make the tomato & apple salsa • Trim and finely dice the tomatoes, apple and onion • Tip into a bowl and add the salt, chilli flakes and vinegar • Squeeze in the juice of the lime • Stir to mix and then add the coriander leaves

Prepare the tacos • Warm the tortillas in a dry pan, in the oven or the microwave and wrap in a clean tea towel to keep warm

Serve up • Cut the lime into wedges • Take all the elements to the table for your guests to build their tacos • Double up 2 tortillas, fold to make a pocket and fill it with rice, chorizo, green beans and salsa • Squeeze over a little more lime and enjoy!

INDIAN SPICED CAULIFLOWER WINGS

A delicious remix of our world-famous buffalo cauliflower wings, this is our take on gobi manchurian, deliciously Indian-spiced fried cauliflower bites. These knobbly, crunchy golden nuggets are the kind of finger food that won't be around for long. They're great on their own, and with the dipping sauce they're downright magnificent. If you've got people coming over, we suggest you make a double batch as these are gonna go down a storm!

Serves 4

1 large cauliflower
2 tsp ground turmeric
1 tbsp salt
vegetable oil, for deep
    frying

For the batter
100g plain flour
50g cornflour
50g rice flour
½ tsp salt

For the sauce
1 tbsp vegetable oil
1 small onion
3 spring onion tops (save
    the bulbs for
    garnishing)
thumb-sized piece
    fresh ginger
6 garlic cloves
2 green chillies
4 tbsp passata
1 tbsp hot sauce
1 tbsp soy sauce
1 tbsp red wine vinegar
1 tbsp sugar

Large saucepan of water on a high heat • Frying pan • Power blender • Deep-sided heavy-based pan • Slotted spoon • Line a tray with kitchen paper

Parboil the cauliflower • Trim the cauliflower and separate it into bite-sized florets • Add the turmeric and salt to the pan of boiling water • Add the cauliflower and boil for 3 minutes • Remove with a slotted spoon and set aside to cool slightly, reserving the water in the pan

Make the batter • Put the flours and salt into a large bowl • Pour in 300–400ml of the turmeric water from the pan and whisk until you have a thick batter that will coat the cauliflower • Tip in the cooled cauliflower florets and mix with a spoon until well coated

Make the sauce • Place the frying pan over a medium heat and add the oil • Peel and slice the onion, slice the spring onion tops and add both to the pan • Fry for 5 minutes, stirring occasionally, until starting to soften • Peel and roughly slice the ginger and garlic and add them to the pan • Trim the chillies, split them down the middle and add them to the pan • Fry for another 5 minutes, stirring now and then, until the garlic is cooked • Add the passata, hot sauce, soy sauce, vinegar and sugar • Simmer for a few minutes and then tip into the blender and blend to a purée • Return to the pan and simmer on the lowest heat • Taste, season and rehydrate with more water if the sauce is too dry

Meanwhile, fry the wings • Place the heavy-based pan over a medium heat • Pour the vegetable oil into the large saucepan so that it comes no more than two-thirds up the side of the pan • Heat the oil to 180°C, or until the oil sizzles around the edges when you dip in a wooden spoon • Fry the cauliflower in batches for 6–8 minutes, until golden brown all over • Transfer to the tray lined with kitchen paper and leave to cool slightly

Serve • Pile the wings on to a serving plate and either drizzle with the hot sauce or serve it in a bowl on the side • Finely slice the spring onion bulbs, sprinkle them over the top and serve

THE NO FOMO BURGER

We've been on a quest to make the perfect vegan chicken burger, and we might just have cracked it! There is no missing out in vegan food, and these burgers should be enough to prove it to anyone who tastes them. They take a little while to make, but by Jove they're worth it. The freeze-and-thaw technique is the best way we've found to maximise marination and get flavour deep into firm tofu, ensuring every bite of your burger is a total taste explosion! Take that, colonel.

Serves 4

600g firm tofu
1 vegan chicken
    stock cube
500ml boiling water
½ tsp garlic powder
½ tsp ground ginger
½ tsp paprika
½ tsp salt
vegetable oil, for frying

For the vegan buttermilk
200ml dairy-free milk
150ml dairy-free yoghurt
1 tbsp white wine vinegar
1 tsp salt

For the spice mix
135g plain flour
135g rice flour
1 tbsp Italian seasoning
1 tbsp ground
    black pepper
1 tbsp fine salt
1 tsp garlic powder
1 tsp ground ginger
½ tsp baking powder
½ tbsp mustard powder
½ tbsp paprika

For the spicy mayo
4 tbsp tomato ketchup
2 tbsp chilli sauce
2 tbsp plant-based mayo
1 tbsp vinegar
½ tsp crushed red chilli
    flakes
pinch of salt

To serve
100g lettuce
4 burger buns (shop-
    bought or
    see opposite)
4 tbsp hot sauce
Kimchi (optional,
    shop- bought
    or see page 173)

Tofu press or 2 clean tea towels and a weight • Freezer-proof containers • Large saucepan • Line a plate with kitchen paper

The day before, prep your tofu • Press the tofu using the tofu press or placed between two clean tea towels with a heavy weight on top

Marinate the tofu • Into a mixing bowl, add the chicken-flavoured stock cube, the water, garlic powder, ground ginger, paprika and salt • Stir to combine, then leave to cool • Pour the stock into a large freezer-proof container • Add the tofu and place in the freezer to freeze completely (at least 2–3 hours) • Remove and defrost completely (at least 2 hours) • Repeat the freezing and defrosting process once more

When you're ready to cook, shape your tofu patties • Press the fully defrosted tofu firmly between two chopping boards to drain all the liquid, being careful not to break it too much • Pat dry with kitchen paper • Carefully cut the tofu into 4 square-shaped patties

Prepare your buttermilk and spice mix • Measure the vegan buttermilk ingredients into a bowl and stir well to combine • Add the spice mix ingredients to a separate bowl and mix well

Double-dip the tofu • Carefully dip a tofu patty into the buttermilk to coat it completely • Transfer to the spice mix and coat completely • Double dip the same patty in the buttermilk and spices • Transfer to a clean plate • Repeat with the other patties

Make your spicy mayo • Measure all the spicy mayo ingredients into a bowl and mix to combine • Shred the lettuce

Fry the patties • Pour the vegetable oil into the large saucepan so that it comes no more than two-thirds up the side of the pan • Heat the oil to 180°C, or until the oil sizzles around the edges when you dip in a wooden spoon • Fry the patties until golden brown, about 5–8 minutes • Transfer to the plate lined with kitchen paper

Build your burgers • Turn on the grill to max • Halve your buns and toast lightly • Spoon 1–2 tablespoons spicy mayo on to the bottom of each bun and top with shredded lettuce • Place a burger on top, then spoon over 1 tablespoon of the hot sauce and a spoonful of kimchi, if using • Cover with the bun tops and serve!

POTATO BURGER BUNS

Makes 6

150g potatoes
1 x 7g sachet fast-action dried yeast
370g strong bread flour
2 tsp sugar
2 tsp sea salt
50ml water
2 tsp dairy-free milk
2 tsp maple syrup
2 tsp white and/or black sesame seeds

Large saucepan of salted water on a high heat • Clean work surface dusted liberally with flour • 1 or 2 clean damp tea towels • Line a baking sheet with parchment paper

Mash the potatoes • Peel the potatoes and cut them into 3cm cubes • Add to the pan of boiling salted water and cook for 10 minutes until tender • Drain, reserving 150ml of the water • Mash the potatoes, then leave them to cool for about 10 minutes to room temperature

Make your dough • Measure the yeast, flour, sugar and salt into a bowl and mix to combine • Add the mashed potato and water • Mix together until a dough forms • Tip the dough on to the prepared surface • Knead for 10–15 minutes, really putting some welly into it, slapping it on the table, quarter-turning it, folding and kneading again • Add a touch more flour if needed to make it less sticky (a wetter dough will give you a fluffier bread) • Place the dough back in the bowl, cover with a damp cloth and leave to prove for 1 hour, until doubled in size

Prepare the toppings • In a small bowl, mix together the milk and maple syrup • Place the sesame seeds in a separate bowl

Shape the buns • Tip the dough back on to the floured work surface and cut it into 6 pieces, about 100g each • Shape each piece into a ball • One by one, dip the tops of the shaped buns into the milk glaze, followed by the sesame seeds, coating the tops • Place on the lined baking sheet and cover with a clean, damp tea towel • Leave to prove for another hour • Preheat the oven to 200°C

Bake the buns • Remove the tea towel and slide the baking sheet into the oven • Bake for 12 minutes, or until the buns are light golden brown and sound hollow when you tap the bottoms • Leave to cool before using

ULTIMATE CHANA MASALA

Chickpea curry is easy to make, but not easy to master. So many chickpea curries in the UK are simply made with onions, spices, tomatoes and chickpeas, and they all come out looking and tasting kind of samey . . . and a bit lazy. THIS is how a good chickpea curry should be made, proper Indian-restaurant style. The teabags and baking soda cook the dried chickpeas perfectly, as well as adding flavour and colour for a rich brown gravy. For a chaat/street-food-style dish, serve with the samosas on page 131 and a topping of vegan yoghurt, Bombay mix and fresh coriander.

Serves 4

200g dried chickpeas
1.5 litres boiling water
2 tea bags
1 tsp salt
¾ tsp baking soda
1 cinnamon stick
4 cloves
4 green cardamom pods

For the spice mix

1 tbsp ground coriander
1 tsp ground cumin
1 tsp ground fenugreek
1 tsp ground ginger
1 tsp ground turmeric
½–1 tsp chilli powder
½ tsp salt
2 tbsp vegetable oil

For the curry

2 tbsp vegetable oil
1 onion
5cm piece fresh ginger
3 garlic cloves
1–2 fresh green chillies
200g dairy-free yoghurt
1 tbsp tomato purée
2 tsp pomegranate
   molasses
½ lemon
1 tsp sugar
1 tbsp dairy-free butter

Soak the dried chickpeas in plenty of cold water overnight • Medium saucepan • Kettle boiled • Sieve • Wok or large frying pan

Cook the chickpeas • Place the saucepan over a high heat • Drain the soaked chickpeas, then tip them into the pan • Pour over the boiling water • Add the tea bags, salt, baking soda and whole spices • Bring to the boil, then reduce to a medium–high heat and cook on a rolling boil until soft, about 75–90 minutes, using a spoon to discard any scum that comes to the surface • Once the chickpeas are cooked, turn the heat off • They should be covered by 1–2cm of water so add a touch more water if needed • Fish out the tea bags, cinnamon stick, cloves and cardamoms and discard (if you can't find the spices it's okay if they stay in)

Meanwhile, prep the rest of the ingredients • Peel and chop the onion very finely • Peel the ginger and cut it in half, slice one half into matchsticks and grate the other • Grate the garlic cloves • Trim and finely slice the chillies • Measure the yoghurt into a small bowl and use a fork to quickly beat it, then pour it through a sieve to remove any lumps • Repeat until the yoghurt is really smooth and liquid

Cook the spice mix • Measure all the spice mix ingredients into a bowl and mix to combine • Place the wok or frying pan on a medium heat and add the 2 tablespoons of oil • Add the spice mix and cook for 2–4 minutes, until the oil is bubbling and the spices have turned a darker brown • Carefully pour the oil and spices into the pan with the chickpeas, being careful not to splash yourself as hot oil and water can spit • Put the pan back on a medium-high heat

Prepare the curry • Add another 2 tablespoons of oil to the pan • Add the onion and cook, stirring frequently, until softened, about 5 minutes • Add the yoghurt, all the ginger, the grated garlic, tomato purée, pomegranate molasses and chillies and stir • Cook for 2 minutes, stirring frequently • Add the spicy chickpeas and liquid from the other pan, squeeze in the lemon juice and add the sugar and dairy-free butter • Mix to combine • Taste and season, adding more salt, lemon juice, chilli powder or coriander to achieve the perfect flavour • Bring to the boil and continue to cook on a medium-high heat, stirring frequently, for 20–30 minutes, until you have a thick, gravy consistency and your chickpeas are cooked through • Spoon into bowls and serve hot

SUPERB SAMOSAS

You really can't beat a good samosa; they're such a joyous thing to chow down on. Glorious golden triangles of crispy pastry filled with delicious, perfectly spiced vegetables and served with a cooling cucumber and mint raita, these are sure to be a hit with anyone you cook them for!

Makes 18 samosas

225g plain flour
1½ tsp sea salt
1½ tbsp vegetable oil
75ml water

For the filling
1 white onion
1 potato (about 150g)
thumb-sized piece
    fresh ginger
2 garlic cloves
1 tsp cumin seeds
1 tsp garam masala
1 tsp ground coriander
pinch of chilli powder
100g frozen peas
150ml water
½ small bunch of
    fresh coriander
salt
500ml–1 litre vegetable
    oil, for deep-frying

For the raita
½ small bunch of
    fresh coriander
½ small bunch of fresh
    mint
200g dairy-free yoghurt
½ lime
salt and black pepper

Medium saucepan with a lid over a medium heat • Clean work surface dusted liberally with flour • Line a baking tray with parchment paper • Large saucepan • Cooking thermometer (optional) • Line a large plate with kitchen paper

Make the filling • Peel and finely chop the onion • Peel the potato and cut it into 1cm cubes • Peel and finely grate the ginger and garlic • Heat 1 tablespoon of the oil in the medium saucepan • Add the onion and fry for 2–3 minutes until softened • Add the ginger, garlic and spices and fry for 2 minutes until fragrant • Add the potatoes, peas and a generous pinch of salt • Stir to mix • Pour in the water • Cover the pan and cook for 13–15 minutes over a medium heat, until the potato is tender • Roughly chop the coriander and fold it in • Taste and season • Crush the potatoes a little with a fork, tip them into a bowl and set them aside to cool to room temperature • Put the bowl in the fridge to chill for 15–20 minutes

Make the dough • Measure the flour and salt into a bowl and stir to combine • Make a well in the centre, add the oil and water and mix • Once the ingredients have come together, tip on to the floured surface and knead for 5–7 minutes until you have a smooth dough • Put the dough back in the bowl, cover and set aside for 30 minutes

Make the raita • Finely chop the coriander • Pick the leaves from the mint and finely chop • Add the herbs, dairy-free yoghurt and the juice of the lime to a bowl and stir to combine • Taste and season with salt and pepper

Fill the samosas • Divide the dough into 9 even balls • Roll each ball into a 12cm circle and cut each circle in half • Take one semicircle and lightly brush the straight edge with water • Bring the two corners of the straight edge together to form a cone, overlapping the edges by about 1cm • Press the overlap together to seal • Spoon 1 tablespoon of the filling into the cone • Pinch the top together to seal • Lay the samosa on the lined tray and repeat to make 18 samosas

Fry the samosas • Pour the vegetable oil into the saucepan so that it comes halfway up the side of the pan • Heat the oil to 180ºC, or until the oil sizzles around the edges when you dip in a wooden spoon • Gently lower 4–5 samosas into the oil and fry for 2–4 minutes until golden, puffed and crispy • Transfer the samosas to the lined plate and repeat until all the samosas are cooked

Serve • Serve immediately with the raita on the side

CHICKPEA CHAAT STREET FOOD BOWL

Serves 1

¼ portion Ultimate Chana Masala (see page 130)
1 or 2 Superb Samosas (see page 131)

To serve
dairy-free yogurt
fresh coriander leaves
sev or Bombay mix (optional)
1 lime

Build your bowl • Spoon a portion of chana masala into a bowl and top with one or two samosas • Drizzle over a dollop of dairy-free yoghurt • Top with some fresh coriander leaves and a generous sprinkling of sev or Bombay mix • Cut the lime in half and squeeze over the juice before serving

MIXED VEG BALTI

Packed with a medley of colourful veg and swimming in a thick, tangy Balti sauce, this brilliant curry uses ingredients we all have lurking in the back of the fridge. Once you've made it a few times you can make it a fridge-raid recipe. Try mixing up the veg and using whatever you have to hand (refer to the chart on page 20–21 for cooking times). Our fiery Chilli & Garlic Naan (page 232) make the perfect accompaniment to this. You'll need to have a batch of Henry's Curry Stock (page 236) ready to go to make this, but if you make a big batch ahead and keep it portioned up in the freezer, you can simply whip it out and quickly defrost it for a speedy punch of flavour.

Serves 4

2 medium potatoes
1 carrot
½ small cauliflower
4 tbsp vegetable oil
1 tsp garam masala
1 onion
2 garlic cloves
5cm piece fresh ginger
1 tomato
1 red pepper
2 fresh chillies
10g fresh coriander
2 tbsp tandoori spice mix
1 tsp ground coriander
1 tsp ground cumin
1 tbsp curry powder
4 tbsp tomato purée
500ml Henry's
    Curry Stock
    (see page 236)
50g frozen peas
1 tbsp cider vinegar
salt

To serve

Chilli & Garlic Naan (see
    page 232, optional)

Make your curry stock (page 236) – if you're using frozen curry stock, defrost it ahead of time • Preheat the oven to 180°C • Saucepan of salted water on a high heat • Baking tray • Large frying pan

Boil your potatoes • Cut the potatoes into 3cm chunks • Add to the pan of boiling salted water and cook for 12 minutes, until knife tender

Meanwhile, prep your veg • Peel and roughly chop the carrot into 2cm chunks • Separate the cauliflower into small 2–3cm florets and chop a few of the leaves into 2–3cm pieces • Tip the carrots and cauliflower florets on to the baking tray and toss with 2 tablespoons of the oil, the garam masala and a little salt • Transfer to the oven and roast for 15 minutes, then add the leaves and roast for a further 10 minutes • Remove when golden brown

Prepare the rest of the ingredients • Peel and chop the onion • Peel and grate the garlic and ginger • Chop the tomato • Cut the pepper into 3cm slices • Trim and finely slice the chillies • Finely chop the fresh coriander

Cook the curry • Pour the rest of the oil into the frying pan and set it over medium heat • Add the onion and a pinch of salt to the hot oil and fry for 3–4 minutes • Add the garlic and ginger and fry for 1 minute • Add the spices and tomato purée and stir for 5–6 minutes, until the mixture is significantly darker and a touch dryer • Add the prepared tomatoes, peppers and chillies • Stir for 2–3 minutes • Add the stock, potatoes, carrot, peas and cauliflower and stir to combine • Simmer for 3–4 minutes until you have a thick gravy • Add the vinegar and stir • Taste and season to perfection • Garnish with the chopped coriander and serve immediately, with the naan, if you like

TOFU MADRAS

This super-spicy Madras features meaty tofu 'steaks' simmered in a spicy tomato and onion broth. There's a fair whack of heat in this one with two teaspoons of chilli powder, which we love, but keep some dairy-free yoghurt on hand to mellow it out if you prefer your curry on the milder side. And don't forget the classic squeeze of lemon to finish – squeeze it in and place it on top! This is one of three curry recipes in this book that use Henry's Curry Stock on page 236 as their base, so we recommend making a big batch of that and keeping it in the freezer ready to pull out for an easy curry night.

Serves 4

350g firm tofu
4 tbsp vegetable oil
1 large brown onion
2 medium tomatoes
3 garlic cloves
3cm piece fresh ginger
10g fresh coriander
2 tbsp tomato purée
500ml Henry's
     Curry Stock
     (see page 236)
¼ lemon

For the tofu coating
½ tsp ground turmeric
1 tsp chilli powder
½ tsp salt
2 tbsp plain flour

For the spice mix
2 tsp chilli powder
1 tsp garam masala
1 tsp salt
½ tsp curry powder
½ tsp ground coriander
½ tsp ground fenugreek
pinch of ground cumin
pinch of ground turmeric

Make your curry stock (page 236) – if you're using frozen curry stock, defrost it ahead of time • Tofu press or 2 clean tea towels and a weight • Large frying pan • Large saucepan

Prep your tofu • Press the tofu for at least 10 minutes using the tofu press or for at least 30 minutes placed between two clean tea towels with a heavy weight on top • Cut the pressed tofu into 5 slices and then cut all the slices in half to make 10 pieces • Measure the coating ingredients into a bowl and mix well • Add the tofu and coat it gently in the spicy flour

Cook the tofu • Place the frying pan over a medium-high heat • Add 2 tablespoons of the oil • Add the tofu steaks to the hot oil and cook until browned on the bottom, about 3–5 minutes • Turn and cook the other side until browned, about 2 minutes • Remove and set aside

Prepare the curry ingredients • Peel and coarsely grate the onion • Trim and chop the tomatoes • Peel and grate the garlic and ginger • Finely chop the coriander • Measure the ingredients for the spice mix into a dish

Cook the curry • Place the saucepan over a medium heat • Add the rest of the oil • Add the spice mix to the hot oil, along with the grated onion and a big pinch of salt • Sauté for 5–7 minutes, stirring frequently, until the fragrances have released • Add the garlic and ginger and cook for 2 minutes • Add the tomato purée, stir and simmer for 2 minutes • Add the chopped tomatoes, stir and simmer for 2 minutes • Add the curry stock and the cooked tofu • Squeeze the lemon juice into the pan and toss in the rind • Reduce the heat to medium-low and simmer for 10 minutes • Taste and adjust the seasoning, adding more garam masala, salt or lemon if needed

Serve • Top with the chopped coriander and serve

TEMPEH VINDALOO

Don't be afraid of this one. Yes, it's spicy, but it also has a beautiful depth of flavour. To do it properly, four teaspoons of chilli powder is the right amount. For a milder but still hot curry, go for two teaspoons. Just make sure it's not extra-hot chilli powder – if it is, tone it down! Like our Madras and Balti recipes, this uses Henry's Curry Stock from page 236 as a base, so making all three curries together and hosting an epic curry night is totally achievable.

Serves 4

1 potato
1 large brown onion
3 large tomatoes
6 garlic cloves
3cm piece fresh ginger
10g fresh coriander
1 tbsp vegetable oil
3 tbsp tomato purée
500ml Henry's
    Curry Stock
    (see page 236)
2 tbsp white-wine vinegar
salt

For the tempeh
400g tempeh
½ tsp salt
1 tsp ground turmeric
½ tsp chilli powder
2 tbsp flour
1 tbsp vegetable oil

For the spice mix
4 green cardamom pods
2 big bay leaves
2–4 tsp hot chilli powder
1 tsp cumin seeds
1 tsp fennel seeds
1 tsp ground coriander
1 tsp ground turmeric
½ tsp black peppercorns
½ tsp garam masala
¼ tsp ground cinnamon

Make your curry stock (page 236) – if you're using frozen curry stock, defrost it ahead of time • Saucepan of salted water with a lid on a high heat • Steamer or heatproof colander • Large frying pan

Prepare your potatoes and tempeh • Cut the potato into 2cm chunks • Cut the tempeh into 2–3cm chunks • Add the potatoes to the pan of boiling salted water • Place the steamer or colander on top, add the tempeh and cover • Cook the potatoes and steam the tempeh for 7 minutes • Remove the tempeh and set aside • Drain the potatoes

Cook the tempeh • Measure the salt, turmeric, chilli powder and flour into a bowl • Stir to combine • Add the steamed tempeh and toss to coat completely • Place a frying pan over a medium-high heat and pour in the vegetable oil • Add the tempeh to the hot oil and fry for about 10 minutes, stirring regularly, until lightly browned • Remove and set aside

Prep the ingredients • Peel and grate the onion • Roughly chop the tomatoes • Peel and grate the garlic and ginger • Finely chop the coriander

Cook the curry • Measure the spice mix into the dry frying pan • Add the tablespoon of oil and place on a medium heat • Cook for 2 minutes, adding half a cup of water to loosen if it gets too dry • Add the grated onion and a pinch of salt • Sauté for 5–7 minutes, stirring frequently, until the fragrances have released • Add the garlic and ginger and cook for 3 more minutes • Add the tomato purée and a large splash of water • Cook for 3 minutes, stirring frequently • Add the stock, vinegar, chopped tomatoes, tempeh and potatoes • Reduce the heat to medium-low and simmer for 10 minutes • Taste and adjust the seasoning, adding more spice mix, salt or vinegar if needed

Serve • Top with the chopped fresh coriander and serve

JACKFRUIT LARB

Is it a salad? Is it a wrap? No. It's larb, and it's here to make your lunchtime tastier. This is a brilliant healthy-but-tasty finger-food meal for when you have friends over and want to put something fun and informal in the middle of the table for everyone to dig into. Great texture, great colour and great taste. What's not to love?

Serves 4 (as a lunch or starter)

2 x 400g tins jackfruit
1 lemongrass stalk
1 garlic clove
2.5cm piece fresh ginger
2–3 red chillies
10g fresh coriander
10g fresh mint
50g salted peanuts
2 baby gem lettuces
1 tbsp groundnut oil

For the dressing
2 limes
1 banana shallot
1 tbsp light soy sauce
1 tbsp sweet chilli sauce

Preheat oven to 200°C • Line a baking tray • Clean tea towel • Pestle and mortar • Wok

Roast the jackfruit • Drain and rinse the jackfruit, then pat dry with the clean tea towel • Spread out on the lined baking tray and roast in the hot oven for 20 minutes • Use two forks to pull apart and shred the jackfruit

Meanwhile, prepare the remaining ingredients • Trim the lemongrass stalk, strip the bark and slice finely • Peel and finely grate the garlic and ginger • Finely slice the chillies • Pick the coriander leaves and finely slice the stems • Pick the mint leaves • Break the peanuts up in the pestle and mortar • Cut away the stems of the lettuce, pull apart the larger leaves and rinse under cold water • Halve the limes for the dressing, peel the shallot, cut it in half and finely slice it lengthways

Cook the larb • Warm the oil in the wok over a medium-high heat • Add the jackfruit and stir for 3–4 minutes • Add the lemongrass, garlic, ginger, two of the chillies and the coriander stems • Stir for 2 minutes • Turn the heat down to very low to keep warm, stirring occasionally to make sure it doesn't catch

Make the dressing • Squeeze the lime juice into a bowl • Add the sliced shallot and squash it slightly to break it down a little • Add the soy sauce and sweet chilli and stir to combine

Serve • Spoon the jackfruit mixture into the lettuce leaves, drizzle over the dressing, garnish with the fresh coriander, mint leaves, broken peanuts and a few slices of chilli if you like it extra kicky! • Serve immediately

CHUNKY MUSHROOM TURKISH PIDE

Pide look like boat-shaped Turkish versions of pizza, their sides gathered up and pinched together to hold a thick layer of delicious filling. In this version, tender mushrooms and red peppers are coated in a smoky harissa sauce that's perfumed with paprika, cumin and garlic. The dough recipe could happily be rolled into a round and repurposed as a pizza base, just top with tomato sauce (see page 83), dairy-free cheese and any other toppings you fancy and bake until crisp.

Serves 4

250g strong white
    bread flour
1 x 7g sachet fast-action
    dried yeast
½ tsp caster sugar
½ tsp salt
150ml warm water
1 tbsp olive oil, plus
    extra for brushing

For the filling
2 red peppers
500g mushrooms
1 tbsp olive oil
big pinch of salt
1 red onion
2 garlic cloves
1–2 tbsp harissa paste
    or tomato paste
1 tbsp smoked paprika
2 tsp ground cumin
small bunch of fresh
    parsley
1 lemon
salt and black pepper

Large mixing bowl and clean work surface dusted liberally with flour or mixer fitted with the dough hook • Large frying pan • Line a large baking sheet • Rolling pin

Make the dough • Add the flour, yeast, sugar and salt to the bowl or mixer and mix to combine • Add the water and the 1 tablespoon oil and mix together • Knead well for 10 minutes either in the mixer or by aggressively bashing the dough on to the floured surface, punching and turning it and folding repeatedly, until smooth and springy • Put in a bowl, cover loosely and leave to rise for 1 hour, or until at least doubled in size

Make the filling • Trim and finely chop the peppers and mushrooms • Place the frying pan over a high heat and add the olive oil • Add the chopped peppers and mushrooms to the hot oil with the salt • Fry for 10 minutes, stirring regularly, until the water has evaporated and the vegetables are cooked down and starting to turn golden • Peel and finely chop half the red onion and add it to the pan • Cook for 5 minutes • Peel and grate the garlic directly into the pan • Add the harissa or tomato paste and stir well, then add the spices and stir again • Remove from the heat • Finely chop half the parsley and stir it through the mixture • Taste and season with salt and pepper • Halve the lemon and squeeze in the juice of half • Set aside to cool

Bake the pides • Heat the oven to 200°C • Tip the risen dough on to a clean surface, roll it into a log and cut it into 4 equal pieces • Roll each piece into an oval about 10cm wide and 20cm long • Transfer to the lined baking sheet • Spoon the filling over the middle of each oval, leaving a 2cm dough border around the edges • Fold the edges up and over the filling around the edges of the pides and pinch together at the ends to create boat shapes • Press a little to make sure the edges stick to the filling and don't flare out during baking • Brush with olive oil and bake for 15–20 minutes, until the dough is deep golden and the bottoms are crisp

Serve • Finely slice the remaining red onion and put the slices into a small bowl • Squeeze over the juice of the lemon half and toss to coat • Pick the parsley leaves and mix them with the lemon and onion • Remove the baked pides from the oven and top them with the onion and parsley mixture • Slice each pide diagonally into 3 pieces and serve

JACK'S WINGS & FRIES

Delicious, breaded jackfruit 'wings', as made famous by London's wonderful Biff's Jack Shack. These are fried until crunchy and golden and served with crisp chips dressed in a punchy coating of jerk seasoning. As if that wasn't enough, we've given you two delicious dipping sauces to serve alongside: the first a gloriously sticky barbecue sauce fragranced with North African Berbere spices, the second full of tropical heat and sweetness in the form of scotch bonnet chillies and pineapple. The only problem is, which to choose?

Serves 4

1 x 560g tin jackfruit
100g strong bread flour
2 tbsp jerk seasoning
  or marinade
20g nutritional yeast
handful of dried
  thyme and/or
  rosemary leaves
1 tsp smoked paprika
2 tbsp soy sauce
2 tbsp olive oil
50g panko breadcrumbs
vegetable oil, for
  deep-frying

For the fries
4 large potatoes
1 tbsp + a pinch of salt
4 tbsp vegetable oil
1 tbsp jerk seasoning

Preheat the oven to 200ºC • **Large baking tray** • **Large saucepan** • **Frying pan** • **Power blender** • **Small saucepan** • **Heavy-based saucepan** • **Line a baking tray with kitchen paper**

Prepare the wings • Drain and rinse the jackfruit thoroughly, then shred it by squishing it between your fingers and breaking it up into small, stringy strands • Place in a bowl and add the flour, jerk seasoning or marinade, nutritional yeast, herbs, paprika, soy sauce and olive oil and combine everything well • Tip the panko into a separate bowl • Shape the jackfruit mixture into 8 'wings' and then dip them in the breadcrumbs, turning them until they are well coated

Make the fries • Cut the potatoes into 1cm fries and tip them into the large saucepan • Cover with water, add a pinch of salt and bring to the boil • Cook for 8–10 minutes, then drain and leave to steam dry • Spread the fries over the baking tray and drizzle with the oil, jerk seasoning and tablespoon of salt • Bake in the hot oven for 30 minutes, shaking the tray regularly to stop the fries sticking

Fry the wings • Pour the vegetable oil into the large saucepan so that it comes no more than two-thirds up the side of the pan • Heat the oil to 180ºC, or until the oil sizzles around the edges when you dip in a wooden spoon • Lower the wings into the oil in batches and deep-fry for about 1–2 minutes, until dark golden brown • Remove to the tray lined with kitchen paper

Serve • Serve the wings with a pile of fries and dishes of each sauce for dipping

BERBERE BBQ SAUCE

Makes enough for all the wings

1 tbsp vegetable oil
½ red or yellow pepper
3 spring onion tops
1 tomato or 1 tbsp
    tomato purée
1 tbsp Berbere spice mix (see page 120)
good pinch of salt
1 tbsp sugar
1 tsp white wine vinegar
1 tbsp BBQ sauce
splash of water

Place a frying pan over a medium heat and add the oil • Seed the pepper • Slice the pepper and spring onion tops and add them to the hot pan • Roughly slice the tomato, if using, and add it or the tomato purée to the pan • Fry everything for 10 minutes, until softened and starting to brown • Add the Berbere spice and salt, stir to mix and cook for another couple of minutes • Add the sugar, vinegar, BBQ sauce and water • Leave to cool slightly before pouring into the blender • Blend until smooth, then set aside to cool

SCOTCH BONNET & PINEAPPLE HOT SAUCE

Makes enough for all the wings

3 scotch bonnets
1 x 430g tin
    pineapple chunks
1 carrot
2 celery sticks
3 cloves
1 tsp salt
2 tbsp malt vinegar
2 tbsp light brown sugar

Seed the chillies and put them in the blender • Drain the pineapple and roughly chop the vegetables • Add them to the blender along with the cloves, salt, malt vinegar and sugar (you might have to do this in batches) • Blend until smooth • Place the small saucepan on a medium heat • Add the hot sauce, bring to the boil and simmer for 20 minutes, or until thickened

AUBERGINE TANDOORI DRUMSTICKS

Aubergines are such wonderful vegetables – you can do so much with them! Here we've roasted them in a deliciously fragrant tandoori marinade and served them in a fluffy naan bread with a cooling kachumber salad, vegan yoghurt dressing and sweet mango chutney. Best served on a summer's evening with good friends and a few cold beers!

Serves 4

For the aubergine
4 small or 2 large
    aubergines
    (about 800g)
2 tbsp fine sea salt

For the tandoori marinade
4 garlic cloves
thumb-sized piece
    of ginger
400g dairy-free yogurt
½ lime
1 tbsp curry powder
1 tsp chilli powder
1 tsp ground ginger
1 tsp ground turmeric
1 tsp mustard seeds

For the kachumber salad
½ onion
1 medium tomato
½ cucumber
½ yellow pepper
½ lime
1 tbsp dried coriander
    or mint, or a mixture
    of both
salt

For the yogurt dressing
½ lemon
200g dairy-free yogurt
½ tsp salt

To serve
4 dairy-free naan breads
4 tbsp mango chutney

Colander • Clean tea towel • Large bowl • Grill tray greased with vegetable oil

Prepare the aubergine • Peel the aubergines and cut them into quarters lengthways • Place in a large colander and pour over the fine sea salt • Mix well with your hands and leave to drain for 10–15 minutes • Rinse under cold water and pat dry with a clean kitchen towel • Heat the grill to max

Make the tandoori marinade • Peel and grate the garlic and ginger into the large bowl and add the rest of the marinade ingredients • Mix well • Add the aubergines and coat them in the marinade

Cook the drumsticks • Spread the aubergine slices evenly over the grill tray • Place under the hot grill and cook for 8–10 minutes • Turn and cook for another 8–10 minutes

Make the kachumber salad • Peel and dice the onion and add to a mixing bowl • Seed and finely dice the tomato, cucumber and pepper and mix with the onion • Add the juice of the lime half and the dried herbs • Season with salt and toss to mix

Make the yogurt dressing • Squeeze the juice of the lemon half into a small bowl • Add the yogurt and salt and stir to combine

Serve • Place the naan under the hot grill and toast for 2 minutes on each side • Pile the kachumber into the middle with 2–4 aubergine drumsticks • Top with the yogurt dressing and some mango chutney and tuck in

ULTIMATE HUMMUS

When we cooked hummus on TV with John Torode, he suggested a few tweaks to our classic recipe. So, we went deep into experimentation mode. This, my friends, is the ultimate silky-smooth hummus, made with cooked chickpeas, which are incredibly affordable. And to up your hummus even further, try our amazing toppings! The Hummus-Bros-style Mexican Beef is made with super-cheap but delicious TVP and is Henry's mum's favourite! And the tabbouleh-inspired salad of herbs, seeds and tomatoes is a plate of delicious green goodness. Enjoy!

Serves 4

250g dried or 2 x 400g tins chickpeas
1 tsp baking soda (if you're using dried chickpeas)
150g runny tahini
80–120ml freshly squeezed lemon juice, to taste
40–80ml extra virgin olive oil, to taste
6 roasted garlic cloves (or 3 raw)
1–2 tsp salt
40–100ml ice-cold water good-quality olive oil, for drizzling (optional)

To serve

topping of your choice (see opposite and over page)
pitta bread, flatbreads, crudités or crisps

Large saucepan (if you're using dried chickpeas) • Food processor

The night before, soak your dried chickpeas, if using • Place the dried chickpeas in a large bowl, cover with water and leave to soak overnight

The next day, cook the soaked chickpeas • Drain the chickpeas and tip them into the large saucepan • Add the baking soda and fill with cold water • Place over a high heat and bring to the boil, then lower to a medium heat and cook for 20–40 minutes, skimming off any foam that rises to the surface • They are done when they are soft to the bite, but not mushy

Blend your hummus • Drain your chickpeas (dried and cooked or tinned) • Keep 1 tablespoon aside and add the rest to the food processor • Add most of the tahini, keeping a couple of tablespoons aside • Add the lemon juice, roasted garlic and salt • Blitz for 2–3 minutes until really smooth • With the processor still running, slowly pour in enough ice-cold water until you have a smooth, creamy, light consistency, thick enough to keep its shape in a bowl but still nice and light and fluffy (bear in mind that it will harden as it cools in the fridge) • Taste and adjust the flavour according to your taste, adding more salt, lemon or garlic as needed to get the flavour perfectly balanced

Serve • Dress with your topping of choice and drizzle over a spoonful of the reserved tahini and a little olive oil • Serve with pitta bread, flatbreads, crudités or crisps

HUMMUS WITH MEXICAN BEEF

Serves 4

1 x portion Ultimate Hummus (see page 150)
960ml boiling water
2 tsp nutritional yeast
1 tbsp + 2 tsp oil
1 tsp miso
1 tsp Marmite
1 tsp sugar
1 vegan beef stock cube
1 tsp salt or smoked salt
12g TVP (textured vegetable protein)
1 garlic clove
2 tbsp tomato purée
salt and black pepper

For the spice mix

6 tsp smoked paprika
2 tsp ground cumin
2 tsp ground coriander
1 tsp chilli powder
salt and black pepper

To serve

chilli flakes
1 tbsp chopped coriander
tortilla chips
nachos or pitta breads
tomato salsa or guacamole

Small saucepan • Place a large bowl in the sink with a colander inside it • Frying pan

Flavour the TVP • Pour the boiling water into the saucepan and stir in the nutritional yeast, the 2 teaspoons of oil, miso, Marmite, sugar, crumbled stock cube and salt • Whisk briefly to combine • Add the TVP and stir, then leave to sit for 20 minutes to rehydrate • Drain the TVP through the colander, catching the stock in the mixing bowl

Make your mince • Place the frying pan over a medium-high heat and add the remaining tablespoon of oil • When it's hot, add the drained TVP and season • Cook, stirring regularly, for 10 minutes, until browned • Crush the garlic into the pan and cook for a further 3 minutes • Remove from the heat • Add the spices for the spice mix and stir well • Cook for 5 minutes, stirring occasionally • Add the reserved stock and tomato purée • Turn the heat up to high and simmer for 10 minutes, stirring regularly, until the liquid has evaporated • Taste and season to perfection

Serve • Measure 2 dessertspoonfuls of hummus into each bowl, using the back of the spoon to create a big swirl with a dip in the middle • Add a quarter of the mince into the dip • Top with some chilli flakes and chopped coriander • Drizzle over the dressing • Serve alongside a handful of tortilla chips, some nachos or pitta breads and either salsa or guacamole

HUMMUS TABBOULEH WITH GARLIC CROÛTONS

Serves 4

1 x portion Ultimate Hummus (see page 150)
250g broccoli
75ml olive oil, plus extra for drizzling
salt and black pepper

For the croûtons
2 garlic cloves
4 tbsp olive oil
4–6 slices fresh bread

For the dressing
1 lemon
150g dairy-free yoghurt
2 tbsp tahini sauce
½ tsp ras el hanout
salt and black pepper

For the salad
2 lemons
1 red onion
1 tbsp ras el hanout
big pinch of salt
small bunch of fresh mint (about 10g)
small bunch of fresh parsley (about 10g)
small bunch of fresh coriander (about 10g)
100g tomatoes

To serve
15g fresh parsley
chilli flakes
tahini sauce

Grill on full whack • Baking tray • Large roasting tin

First, grill your broccoli • Cut the big stem off the broccoli, quarter it then cut it into 5mm slices • Cut small florets about 2½cm • Place the broccoli on the baking tray and sprinkle with salt, pepper and olive oil • Place under the hot grill to cook for 3–5 minutes, turning occasionally, until softened, checking regularly so as not to burn them • Set aside to cool

Next, make your croûtons • Crush the garlic into the roasting tin and add the oil and a little salt and pepper • Stir to mix • Cut the bread into 2½cm chunks and add them to the tin • Toss well • Slide the tin under the grill to toast for 2–4 minutes until golden brown, checking and turning frequently to make sure the croûtons don't burn • Set aside to cool

Make your dressing • Grate the zest into a bowl, then halve the lemon and squeeze in the juice • Add all the remaining dressing ingredients and whisk to combine

Make your salad • Halve the lemons and squeeze the juice into a large bowl • Peel and finely chop the red onion and add it to the bowl • Add the ras el hanout and a big pinch of salt • Squeeze the onion with your fingers so the lemon starts to pickle it • Remove and discard the stems from the mint and any thicker stems from the parsley and coriander • Finely chop the leaves and fine stems and add them to the bowl • Finely chop the tomatoes and add them to the bowl along with the sliced broccoli stems

Serve • Measure 2 dessertspoonfuls of hummus into each bowl, using the back of the spoon to create a big swirl of hummus with a dip in the middle • Add a quarter of the herby salad into the dip and top with the grilled broccoli • Drizzle over the dressing and a little tahini sauce, and top with a few fresh parsley leaves and a scattering of chilli flakes • Serve with your garlic croûtons alongside

TEENIE TINY TATER TOTS

Delightful little nuggets of fried potato that are deliciously crispy on the outside, but oh so fluffy on the inside. If you're looking to up your sides game, these are a great alternative to regular old fries! We've also given you a recipe for your own Tommy K, which ditches the artificial sweetness of shop-bought versions!

Serves 4

For the Tater Tots
1kg Maris piper or other
    floury potatoes
1 tbsp plain flour
1 tsp garlic powder
½ tsp onion granules
¼ tsp Italian herbs
fresh chives (optional)
salt and black pepper
vegetable oil, for
    deep-frying

For the Tommy K
1 onion
2 garlic cloves
1 tbsp vegetable oil
½ tsp cayenne pepper
¼ tsp ground cinnamon
2 whole cloves
350g passata
60g brown sugar
75ml malt vinegar

Large saucepan with a lid over a medium heat • Power blender • Large saucepan • Clean tea towel • Deep-sided frying pan • Cooking thermometer (optional) • Line a large plate with kitchen paper

Make the Tommy K • Peel and finely dice the onion • Peel and grate the garlic cloves • Pour the oil into the hot saucepan • Add the onions and stir-fry for 7–10 minutes, until golden brown • Add the garlic, cayenne pepper, cinnamon, whole cloves and passata and stir for another 4–5 minutes • Add the sugar and vinegar and stir until the sugar is dissolved • Cover the pan and simmer for 30 minutes • Take off the heat and leave to cool to room temperature • Transfer to a blender and whizz until completely smooth

Meanwhile, prepare the potatoes • Peel the potatoes and put them in a large pan • Cover with cold water, bring to the boil over a high heat and cook for 6–7 minutes • Drain and leave to steam dry • Lay the tea towel out on the kitchen counter and grate the cooled potatoes into the middle of the towel • Bring up the corners of the towel and squeeze out as much water as you can

Shape the Tater Tots • Put the grated potatoes, flour, garlic powder, onion granules, Italian herbs, salt and pepper into a bowl and work them with your hands to combine • Squeeze the potatoes into stubby 2cm tube shapes

Fry the tater tots • Pour the oil into the frying pan until it's 5cm deep • Put the pan over a medium heat and heat to 180°C or until the oil sizzles around the edges when you dip in a wooden spoon • Add 5 Tater Tots to the pan and fry for 4–5 minutes, until golden and crispy • Transfer to the lined plate to drain • Repeat until all the Tater Tots are cooked

Serve • Season the Tater Tots with salt and pepper • Garnish with fresh chives, if using, and serve immediately with the Tommy K on the side

COMFORT

BIG-BATCH BOLOGNESE SAUCE

We've written a fair few bolognese recipes over the years, but this one, made with celeriac and lentils, is one of our best. Be warned though, it makes a BIG batch! One portion of this will happily feed sixteen people, but it freezes like a dream. Having a few portions in your freezer is a great idea as it means you'll have something delicious to eat even if you don't fancy cooking from scratch!

Makes about 4kg

200g red lentils
1 large white onion
1 celeriac (about 500g trimmed weight)
1 leek
2 celery sticks
600g mushrooms
6 garlic cloves
handful of parsley stalks
1 tbsp olive oil
4 tbsp tomato purée
4 tbsp balsamic vinegar
100ml wine (optional)
1 litre vegetable stock
4 x 400g tins basic chopped tomatoes
2 x cinnamon sticks
2 bay leaves
6 sprigs of fresh thyme
salt and black pepper

Large food processor • **Large saucepan with a lid** • **Freezer bags or containers** •

Soak the lentils • Tip the lentils into a bowl and cover with cold water • Set aside

Prepare the veg • Trim and roughly chop the onion, celeriac, leek, celery and mushrooms • Peel the garlic • Add the onion and celeriac to the processor with half the mushrooms • Pulse until you have rough dice , then tip into a bowl • Add the onion, leek, celery, garlic and parsley to the processor with the rest of the mushrooms • Pulse to chop, then add to the bowl with the onion and celeriac • Continue in batches until all the vegetables are chopped • Stir to combine

Cook the veg • Place the pan over a medium heat and add the olive oil • Once the oil is hot, add the chopped veg, stir, cover and cook over a low heat for 20 minutes, stirring occasionally, then remove the lid • Add the tomato purée and balsamic vinegar, scraping the bottom of the pan to get any tasty bits of caramelised veg off the bottom • Add the wine (if using), stock, chopped tomatoes, cinnamon sticks, bay and thyme • Season generously • Simmer for 30 minutes • Drain the lentils and add them to the pan, cover and cook for another 10–15 minutes, until the lentils are cooked • Taste and adjust the seasoning, adding more balsamic if you want more sweetness and acidity • Remove the cinnamon sticks and bay leaves and you're good to go!

Store • Allow the bolognese to cool and then portion up and freeze lying flat as this makes it super quick to defrost when you want a quick supper

SPAGHETTI BOLOGNESE

Once you've made the Big-Batch Bolognese Sauce (opposite), it's the work of moments to knock up a delicious spag bol. We like to freeze our bolognese sauce in smallish portions, so can easily whip enough for just one or two people out of the freezer without any going to waste.

See below for servings

125g bolognese
    per person
100g spaghetti
    per person
dairy-free
    Parmesan
1 lemon
fresh thyme or
    oregano leaves
salt

If you're using frozen batch bolognese, defrost it in the fridge overnight • Large saucepan of salted water on a high heat • Large frying pan on a medium heat (if you're reheating cold sauce)

Prepare the sauce • Make the bolognese following the method above or tip your defrosted portions into the frying pan and warm gently

Cook your pasta • Add the pasta to the pan of boiling salted water and cook until al dente, following the instructions on the packet

Serve • Once the pasta is cooked, transfer it to the bolognese pan, bringing some of the pasta water with it • Stir to coat • Divide the spaghetti between bowls and grate over some dairy-free Parmesan, the zest from the lemon and sprinkle with the fresh herbs

SUPER-EASY LASAGNE

Everyone loves lasagne, but doing it properly takes a long time (our Frying Pan Lasagne from *Speedy BOSH!* excluded!). If you have a half-batch of Big-Batch Bolognese (see opposite) ready to go, putting this together is just a case of making a béchamel, layering up the lasagne sheets and baking it till it's golden and bubbling. Yum!

Serves 6

1½kg Big-Batch
    Bolognese
    (see opposite)
300g egg-free
    lasagne sheets
handful of fresh chives
dairy-free Parmesan
    (optional)

For the béchamel
100g dairy-free butter
100g plain flour
1 litre dairy-free milk
2 tsp English or
    wholegrain mustard
2 tsp bouillon or stock
2 tbsp nutritional yeast
2 tsp white wine vinegar
a few gratings of nutmeg
salt and black pepper

If using frozen bolognese, defrost it in the fridge overnight • Preheat the oven to 200°C • 20 x 30cm lasagne dish • Small pan over a low heat

Make the béchamel • Melt the dairy-free butter in the small pan • Add the flour and whisk to combine • Slowly add the milk, whisking out any lumps • Add the mustard, bouillon or stock, nutritional yeast, vinegar and the nutmeg • Season to taste • Cook until thickened to the consistency of double cream, then take off the heat

Build your lasagne • Ladle a thin layer of bolognese into the dish • Top with a thin layer of béchamel and cover with a single layer of lasagne sheets • Repeat until all the ingredients are used up, finishing with a layer of pasta topped with béchamel • Snip the chives over the top and sprinkle with a good grating of dairy-free Parmesan

Bake the lasagne • Transfer the dish to the hot oven and bake for 30–35 minutes, until bubbling and brown on top • Remove and leave to rest for 10–15 minutes before serving

FIERY 5 BEANS & GRAINS CHILLI

The clever thing about this chilli is that we cook the grain in the chilli, so you don't have to worry about cooking a separate batch of rice to serve it with. Serve with a dollop of salsa or guacamole and you're in for the win!

Serves 4

1 x 400g tin or 100g
   dried pinto beans
1 x 400g tin or 100g
   dried haricot beans
1 x 400g tin or 100g
   dried kidney beans
1 large white onion
1 medium carrot
1 large celery stick
2 Portobello or 125g
   regular mushrooms
3 tbsp vegetable oil
4 garlic cloves
1 small bunch of
   fresh coriander
3 tbsp smoked paprika
1 tbsp chipotle paste
2 tbsp tomato purée
200g pearl barley
1 x 400g tin
   chopped tomatoes
1 tbsp apple cider vinegar
1 litre vegetable stock
150g coarse bulgur wheat
salt and black pepper

For the ancho chilli

1 dried ancho chilli
60ml ground or
   instant coffee
1 tsp maple syrup
   or caster sugar

To serve

100g pumpkin seeds
pinch of sea salt
1 lime

The night before: Pour the dried beans, if using, into a large bowl • Cover with plenty of water and leave to soak overnight •

On the day: Large stock pot • Small frying pan

Cook the dried beans, if using • Drain the soaked beans and cook in fresh water according to the packet instructions until tender

Soak the ancho chilli • Prepare the coffee in a mug • Stir in the maple syrup • Submerge the chilli in the coffee and set aside

Prepare the base vegetables • Peel and finely dice the onion • Peel, trim and dice the carrot • Trim and dice the celery • Roughly chop the mushrooms into 1cm pieces • Place the stock pot over a medium heat and pour in the vegetable oil • Add the onion, carrot and celery to the pan with a pinch of salt • Cook for 10 minutes, stirring occasionally

Add the herbs and spices • Meanwhile, peel and grate the garlic cloves • Rip the leaves from the coriander, set them to one side and finely slice the stems • Add the garlic to the pot and stir for 2 minutes • Add the paprika, chipotle paste, tomato purée and coriander stems and stir for 1 minute • Fish out the ancho chilli, finely slice it and add it to the pan, reserving the coffee • Drain and rinse the beans • Add them to the pot with the pearl barley, chopped tomatoes, reserved coffee, apple cider vinegar and 600ml of the vegetable stock so that the beans are covered by 2–3cm of liquid • Stir • Increase the heat so the chilli is simmering gently • Put the lid on slightly askew to leave a gap at the top and cook for 30 minutes, stirring occasionally

Add the bulgur wheat • Add the bulgur wheat and another 300ml of the stock • Stir and put the lid back on tightly • Simmer for 10 minutes

Toast the pumpkin seeds • Pour the seeds and a generous pinch of sea salt into the dry frying pan and place over a medium heat • Toast until slightly darkened and beginning to pop • Transfer to a bowl to cool

Finish the chilli • Test the chilli and if the grains are still a little firm, add the remaining stock, put the lid on and simmer for a few more minutes • Taste and season with salt and pepper

Serve • Cut the lime into wedges • Spoon the chilli into bowls, sprinkle with some of the pumpkin seeds and the reserved coriander leaves • Serve immediately, with the lime wedges alongside for squeezing

BAKED RATATOUILLE RICE

In the BOSH! kitchen, we always find simple ratatouille to be a little boring as a dish, and we wanted to make something truly outstanding. This baked ratatouille rice is perhaps the finest baked rice we've ever tasted! First we use confit tomatoes, garlic and herbs with oil, before adding a wonderful selection of veg and rice to create a perfectly flavoured all-in-one dish. This Mediterranean-flavoured dish tastes as good as it looks.

Serves 4

1 large red onion
650g cherry tomatoes
12 large or 25 small
    garlic cloves
15g fresh parsley
½ tsp ground cinnamon
½ tsp ground fennel
½ tsp Italian herbs
½ tsp salt
½ tsp pepper
100ml olive oil
1 aubergine
1 courgette
1 vegetable stock cube
2 tbsp tomato purée
600ml boiling water
300g basmati rice
4–5 medium tomatoes
salt and black pepper

To serve
green salad

Preheat the oven to 180°C · 20 x 30cm lasagne or roasting dish · Kettle boiled · Heatproof jug · Tin foil

Prepare the base · Peel, halve and slice the onion · Halve the cherry tomatoes · Peel and slice the garlic · Pick the parsley leaves and set them to one side · Add the onion, tomatoes, garlic, parsley stems, cinnamon, fennel, Italian herbs, salt, pepper and olive oil to the roasting dish and gently stir everything together · Put the dish in the oven and roast for 50 minutes

Prepare the topping vegetables · Trim the aubergine and courgette and cut into 3–4mm rounds · Cut the medium tomatoes into 5mm thick slices

Carry on cooking · Remove the dish from the oven and increase the temperature to 220°C · Add the stock cube, tomato purée and boiling water to a jug and stir until the stock cube has dissolved · Sprinkle the rice evenly over the roasting dish · Gently pour in the stock to cover the rice · Arrange the aubergine, courgette and tomato slices over the rice in sequence, working in a spiral from the outside to the middle, until the rice is completely covered · Season with salt and pepper, seal the dish tightly with tin foil, put it in the oven and roast for 15 minutes

Finish the dish · Take the dish out of the oven and carefully remove the foil (watch out for steam) · Turn the grill to max and put the dish underneath · Grill for 10–15 minutes, until the top has turned golden and lightly crispy

Serve · Garnish with the parsley leaves · Spoon into serving dishes and serve immediately with a simple green salad

SWEDISH MEATBALLS, MASH & GRAVY

These deliciously meaty vegan meatballs are made with plant-based sausages, butter beans and breadcrumbs. So warming and comforting, you're gonna love them!

Serves 4

125g bread
1½ tins butter beans
(about 345g
drained weight)
3½ tbsp vegetable oil,
plus extra for greasing
1 tsp Marmite
¼ tsp white or ½ tsp
black pepper
1 tsp dried thyme
1 onion
250g plant-based
sausages, at room
temperature

For the gravy

1 onion
1 tbsp vegetable oil
½ tin butter beans (about
115g drained weight)
20g tahini
¼ tsp white or ½ tsp
black pepper
300ml dairy-free barista-
style milk
100ml water
pinch of nutmeg
1 tsp dried thyme
20g Marmite
1 bay leaf
½ lemon
½ tsp sugar
salt and black pepper

For the mash

6-8 floury potatoes
(about 800g)
2 tbsp dairy-free butter
70ml oat milk
salt and black pepper

To serve

3 sprigs of fresh dill

Food processor • **Line a baking tray with parchment paper** • **Frying pan** • **Medium saucepan with lid** • **Wide shallow casserole**

Make the meatballs • Add the bread to the food processor and pulse to breadcrumbs • Transfer to a mixing bowl • Rinse the butter beans under cold water and add half to the processor with 1½ tablespoons of the oil, the Marmite, pepper and thyme • Blitz until smooth • Scrape the mixture into the mixing bowl • Peel and quarter the onion and put it in the processor • Pulse until finely chopped and add to the bowl • Add the remaining butter beans and the sausages to the processor, pulse until roughly chopped, then transfer to the bowl • Fold everything together until evenly combined • Lightly oil your hands and shape the mixture into about 20 balls • Place on the lined baking tray and freeze for 20 minutes

Start the gravy • Preheat the oven to 160°C and place the frying pan over a medium heat • Peel, halve and finely slice the onion • Warm the vegetable oil in the frying pan • Add the onions and a pinch of salt and stir for 8-10 minutes until the onions are golden • Transfer to a plate

Meanwhile, start the mash • Peel and chop the potatoes into 2.5cm chunks • Transfer to the saucepan, add a pinch of salt and cover with cold water • Bring to the boil and simmer for 12-15 minutes until tender

Cook the meatballs • Add 2 more tablespoons of oil to the frying pan and place it over a medium heat • Transfer half the meatballs to the pan to fry for 3-4 minutes until golden • Transfer to a plate • Add more oil and repeat to cook the remaining meatballs • Put all the meatballs back on the baking tray, put the tray in the oven and bake for 20 minutes

Finish the potatoes • Drain the potatoes and tip them back into the pan • Add the dairy-free butter and milk, season, and mash until creamy • Put the lid on the pan and turn the heat down very low to keep warm

Finish the gravy • Wipe the food processor clean • Add the butter beans, tahini, pepper, milk, water, nutmeg, thyme and Marmite and blitz until smooth • Transfer the mixture to the casserole dish along with the bay leaf • Place over a medium heat until just simmering • Add the onion • Squeeze in the lemon juice • Add the sugar and stir to combine • Taste and season • Leave to simmer and thicken for 4-5 minutes

Time to serve • Pick the dill fronds from the sprigs • Transfer the meatballs to the casserole dish and garnish with the dill • Spoon the mashed potato into serving bowls • Top the potato with the meatballs and gravy and serve immediately

THRIFTY ROAST DINNER

A delicious, hearty Sunday roast with all the trimmings on a budget – not possible, surely! Well, not only have we created one for you, but it's a true feast that will leave your table groaning with dishes and your guests salivating in anticipation. A soft and supple whole roasted celeriac, gloriously garlicky roasties, braised cabbage, roasted glazed onions and carrots, and both gravy and bread sauce. Remember to save room for dessert. Then make some time for a nap!

Serves 4

For the celeriac
1 large celeriac
50ml vegetable oil
2 garlic cloves
2 sprigs of fresh thyme
1½ tbsp Marmite
1 tsp olive oil
2 tsp maple syrup
1½ tbsp nigella seeds

For the bread sauce
½ small onion
4 cloves
500ml oat milk
2 sprigs fresh thyme
1 bay leaf
100g breadcrumbs
salt and black pepper

For the roast potatoes
1kg potatoes
1 vegetable stock cube
4 garlic cloves
4 tbsp olive oil
salt and black pepper

For the onions and carrots
500g carrots
350g small onions
2 tbsp olive oil
2 garlic cloves
1 tbsp maple syrup
4 sprigs of fresh thyme
salt and black pepper

For the gravy
1 bay leaf
350ml vegetable stock
1 tbsp plain flour
2 tbsp Marmite
salt and black pepper

For the cabbage
1 small savoy cabbage
1 tbsp red wine vinegar
salt and black pepper

Preheat the oven to 200°C • Metal skewer • Frying pan on a medium-high heat • Tin foil • Small roasting tin • Small saucepan • Large saucepan • Two large roasting tins • Medium saucepan

Sear the celeriac • Peel the celeriac, removing all the dark knobbly bits and making it as smooth as possible • Pierce it all over with a metal skewer • Pour the vegetable oil into the frying pan so that it's 1cm deep • Add the garlic (skins on) and 1 sprig of the thyme and fry for 3 minutes until golden brown, then remove and discard • Place the celeriac in the pan and sear the bottom until it's a caramel colour • Carefully baste the top with the herb oil • Carefully turn the celeriac in the oil to colour it all over a dark caramel colour (this will take about 10 minutes. You can insert the skewer into the celeriac to help you turn it) • Take the celeriac out of the pan and leave it to rest for 2 minutes • Season with salt and pepper

Glaze and roast the celeriac • Mix together the Marmite, olive oil and maple syrup in a small bowl • Cut a large square of tin foil and lay it in the small roasting tin • Place the celeriac in the middle of the foil and brush it with half the Marmite glaze • Bring the edges of the foil up around the celeriac, leaving a small gap at the top and making sure the foil isn't touching its edges • Put the tin in the oven and roast for 1–1½ hours

Start the bread sauce • Peel the onion and spike it with the cloves • Place in the small saucepan and add the oat milk, thyme and bay leaf • Place the pan over a medium-low heat and simmer gently for 30 minutes

Prepare the roast potatoes • Peel and halve the potatoes • Place them in the large saucepan and crumble over the stock cube, cover with water and add a generous pinch of salt • Put the pan over a high heat and bring to the boil • Immediately reduce the heat and simmer for 8-10 minutes, until the potatoes are tender • Drain in a colander and leave to steam dry, then toss to 'chuff' the potatoes • Tip them into a large roasting tin • Add the garlic cloves • Drizzle with the olive oil, season with salt and pepper and toss to coat • Cover and set aside

Prepare the onions and carrots • Peel the carrots, cut them into 5cm pieces and place them on one side of the second roasting tin • Peel and halve the onions and place them in the other half of the tin, cut-side up • Season with salt and pepper, add the garlic cloves and drizzle with the olive oil

Roast the vegetables • Place the potatoes in the oven and roast for 45 minutes • Place the onions and carrots in the oven and roast for 30 minutes

Finish the bread sauce • Remove the onion and herbs from the pan and discard • Add the breadcrumbs to the milk, season with salt and pepper, fold to combine and leave to soak for 20 minutes

Finish the celeriac • Pick the leaves from the remaining thyme sprig • Remove the celeriac from the oven and carefully loosen the foil (being careful not to scald yourself with the steam) • Brush the celeriac with the remaining glaze • Sprinkle with the nigella seeds and thyme leaves • Put the tin back in the oven and roast the uncovered celeriac for another 10–15 minutes

Finish the roast vegetables • Remove the tray of onions and carrots from the oven • Transfer a quarter of the onions to a chopping board • Drizzle the maple syrup over the carrots and onions and lay the thyme sprigs on top • Return the tray to the oven • Take the tin of roast potatoes out of the oven and transfer the garlic cloves to the chopping board • Return the tray to the oven

Make the gravy • Carefully pop all the garlic cloves out of their skins • Roughly chop the onion and garlic and transfer them to the medium saucepan • Place the pan over a medium heat • Add the bay leaf and stock and simmer for 10 minutes • Mix the flour and Marmite together in a small bowl and add the mixture to the pan • Whisk to combine and simmer for a further 5 minutes • Taste and season with salt and pepper

Steam the cabbage • Quarter, core and roughly cut the cabbage into long, thick strands • Transfer to a colander and place on top of the gravy pan • Put the saucepan lid over the colander and leave the cabbage to steam

Serve • Reheat the bread sauce, adding a splash of water to loosen it if needed • Remove the celeriac from the oven and cut it into quarters • Plate up the celeriac, roast potatoes, onions, carrots and bread sauce • Take the lid off the cabbage, season it with salt and pepper, drizzle over the red wine vinegar and transfer to the plates • Sieve the gravy to remove any lumps and serve immediately

KIMCHI UDON NOODLES

Kimchi is said to be good for gut health and has such a unique sharp, spicy flavour. We absolutely love it, so we decided to give it pride of place in its very own recipe! Simple, yet ever-so-satisfying, it really is a great place to start if you've never tried kimchi before. The crunchy texture of the carrots complements the soft, silky texture of the udon noodles, and the zippiness of the sauce will definitely tick your boxes if you're into big flavours. If you want to make this using your own kimchi (see overleaf) then you'll need to get started a few days ahead.

Serves 2

280g firm tofu
2 tbsp cornflour
2 carrots
200g spring greens
2 spring onions
2 garlic cloves
3 heaped tbsp Kimchi (see page 173)
2 tbsp vegetable oil
300g straight-to-wok udon noodles
2 tsp toasted sesame seeds

For the sauce
1 tbsp gochujang paste
1 tbsp toasted sesame oil
2 tsp soy sauce
1 tsp maple syrup

Tofu press or 2 clean tea towels and a weight • Kettle boiled • Wok • Plate lined with kitchen paper

Prepare the tofu • Press the tofu for at least 10 minutes using the tofu press or for at least 30 minutes placed between two clean tea towels with a heavy weight on top • Cut into 2cm pieces • Add to a bowl with the cornflour and toss to coat

Prepare the vegetables • Peel the carrots and cut them into thin strips • Trim, core and finely shred the spring greens • Trim and finely slice the spring onions • Peel and grate the garlic • Squeeze the juice of the kimchi into a small bowl and set the bowl to one side • Finely chop the kimchi

Prepare the sauce • Measure all the sauce ingredients into the bowl with the kimchi juice and stir to combine

Stir-fry • Place the wok over a medium-high heat and add the oil • Add the tofu pieces to the hot oil and fry for 3-4 minutes, until golden and crispy, then transfer to the plate lined with kitchen paper • Add the carrots to the wok and stir-fry for 1 minute • Add the spring greens and stir-fry for 2 minutes • Add the garlic and chopped kimchi and stir-fry for 1 minute

Add the noodles • Pour the boiling water over the noodles to wake them up, then shake off the water • Add the noodles and tofu to the wok and stir to combine • Turn down the heat, add the sauce and toss to combine

Serve • Plate up the kimchi noodles, dress with the spring onions and sesame seeds and serve immediately

KIMCHI

Kimchi recipes are hit and miss, with many missing the flavour that we look for: spicy, rich and packed with umami, fire and seasoning. This recipe is absolutely banging, and we'd be happy to volunteer it for a taste test against any competitor. Having a jar of kimchi ready to go in the fridge is a great way to add an instant punch of fiery flavour to any dish. It's wonderful added to a stir fry, stirred into a spicy stew or spooned into a sandwich or burger. Because it's fermented, it's also great for gut health and is a great way of using up veg that's past its best. It also lasts for ages and, kept in the fridge, will be good for around 3 months.

Makes 1 large or several small jars

2 napa or Chinese cabbages
50g salt for every litre or water (see recipe)
100g carrot
200g radish
5 spring onions

For the paste
30g fresh pear
10g fresh ginger
10g garlic cloves
30g onion
2 tbsp maple syrup
1½ tbsp gochujang paste
1 tbsp vinegar
1 tbsp chilli flakes
2 tsp salt

Sterilise your jars, lids and all your equipment by washing them in hot soapy water, rinsing in boiling water and then draining them on a clean tea towel until they're completely dry • Large mixing bowl • Small plate that fits inside the bowl • Thermometer • Medium saucepan of water at 50°C • Weighing scales • Cling film • Blender • Large storage container

Prepare the cabbage • Quarter the cabbages lengthways and cut out the cores • Cut into 3cm thick shreds and put them in a bowl • Put the bowl on the scales and note the weight • Pour over enough of the warm water to just submerge the cabbage, making a note of how much water you've added • Add 50g salt for every litre of water you poured into the bowl • Cover the cabbage with cling film, pressing it down into the bowl, and place a small plate on top • Place a small weight such as a glass tumbler on the plate to weigh down the cabbage and keep it submerged • Leave for 4–6 hours until the cabbage is firm and crunchy

Prepare the rest of the vegetables • Peel, trim and grate the carrot • Trim and grate the radishes • Slice the white part of the spring onions and shred the green part

Prepare the paste • Peel and core the pear • Peel the ginger, garlic and onion • Place all the paste ingredients into the blender and blitz until smooth

Combine the elements • Clean your hands thoroughly • Drain the cabbage well, then tip it into a bowl with the prepared vegetables and paste and stir to combine • Transfer the kimchi to the container • Lay cling film on top and place a weight (such as a flat-bottomed tumbler) on top • Leave to ferment for 24–36 hours at about 20°C

Time to store • Remove the weight and cling film and stir the kimchi • Cover the jar and put it in the fridge to chill, ready to use

JANE'S SPANISH STEW

Henry's mum, Jane, taught him the delights of simple Spanish flavours when he was young. This hearty stew of creamy beans, sweet red peppers and tender chunks of sausage in a vibrant sauce will take you right back to long, lazy summer days. As if that wasn't enough, we've added our ultimate garlic loaf for ripping and dunking. Dinner, just like Jane used to make.

Serves 4

1 tbsp cooking oil
1 large onion
2 garlic cloves
3 sprigs fresh thyme
    or ¾ tsp dried
1½ tsp sweet
    smoked paprika
1 tsp ground coriander
¾ tsp fennel seeds
2 tbsp tomato purée
1 x 400g tin chopped
    tomatoes
700ml water
2 red peppers,
    thinly sliced
1 x 400g tin butter beans
1 x 400g tin haricot beans
2 lemons
15g fresh parsley,
    finely chopped
    (optional)
½ orange
salt and black pepper

For the sausages

8 plant-based sausages
    at room temperature
¼ tsp black peppercorns
2 sprigs fresh thyme
    or ¾ tsp dried
1 tbsp cooking oil
½ tsp cayenne pepper
½ tsp ground coriander
½ tsp sweet
    smoked paprika

For the ultimate
garlic loaf
1 garlic bulb
1 tsp vegetable oil
¼ tsp fennel seeds
¼ bunch of fresh parsley
100g dairy-free butter
1 x 800g tiger
    bread bloomer
salt and black pepper

Preheat the oven to 200°C • Line a large baking sheet • Deep heavy-based frying pan or casserole with a lid over a medium-low heat • Cut a square of tin foil big enough to wrap the garlic bulb • Roasting tin

Make the stew • Pour the oil into the hot pan • Peel and finely chop the onion and add it to the pan • Cover and cook, stirring now and again, for 8–10 minutes, until softened and lightly golden • Crush the garlic • Pick the thyme leaves, if needed • Remove the lid from the pan and add the garlic, spices and thyme • Stir-fry for 1 minute • Add the tomato purée, tinned tomatoes and water • Bring to the boil and leave to bubble for 5 minutes • Trim and thinly slice the red peppers and add them to the pan • Reduce the heat to a gentle simmer, cover and cook for 20 minutes • Drain the beans • Take the lid off the pan, add the beans and increase the heat • Bring back to the boil and cook for 5 minutes • Lower the heat and simmer for 10 minutes

Roast the garlic for the garlic loaf • Remove 2 cloves of garlic from the bulb and set them aside • Place the rest of the bulb in the centre of the foil square • Drizzle with the vegetable oil, fennel seeds and a little salt • Wrap tightly and place in the hot oven for 20 minutes

Cook the sausages • Cut the sausages into chunks • Crack the peppercorns • Pick the leaves from the thyme • Put the sausage chunks in the roasting tin and sprinkle over the oil, spices and thyme • Mix to coat the sausages well • When the garlic has been in the oven for 20 minutes, turn down the heat to 140°C • Put the roasting tin alongside the garlic package and bake for 20 minutes more

Finish the garlic bread • Take the garlic package out of the oven and open it up to let out the steam • Finely chop the parsley, if using • Once the garlic is cool, unwrap the cloves and squeeze the flesh into a bowl • Add the parsley, black pepper and butter • Mix until smooth • Make a few cuts in the bread, slicing a third of the way into the loaf • Spread the garlic butter into the cracks • Place on the lined baking tray and warm in the oven for 10 minutes

Serve • Halve one of the lemons and squeeze the juice into the stew • Cut the other lemon into wedges • Finely chop the parsley, if using • Squeeze the juice of the orange over the stew • Season well and sprinkle with the chopped parsley • Dot the sausage chunks on top • Serve with the ultimate garlic loaf and the lemon wedges on the side

TAKE-A-BREAK BAKES

These are a plant-based version of the steak bakes you often find in high-street bakeries. We've served them with roasted veg and extra gravy for a warming and substantial meal. Once assembled, these freeze brilliantly and simply need to be defrosted and baked off for an easy-win dinner.

Serves 4

400g mushrooms
1 medium carrot
450ml boiling water
1 vegan stock cube
2 tbsp soy sauce
2 garlic cloves
2 tbsp olive oil
10g fresh parsley
2 rolls dairy-free
    puff pastry
2 tbsp oat milk
½ tsp brown sugar
salt and black pepper

For the gravy
1 white onion
2 tbsp olive oil
2 tbsp nutritional yeast
1 tsp onion powder
50ml stout or beer
1 bay leaf
2 tbsp cornflour
2 tbsp water
salt and black pepper

Preheat the oven to 200°C • Line 3 baking sheets with parchment paper • Small saucepan over a medium heat

Prepare the filling • Cut the mushrooms into 1cm pieces • Peel and dice the carrot • Pour the boiling water into a bowl and stir in the stock cube and soy sauce • Add the chopped mushroom and carrot and leave to soak for 5 minutes • Transfer the soaked vegetables to one of the baking trays, reserving the marinade • Put the tray in the oven and roast for 25 minutes • Remove and transfer the vegetables to a clean bowl to cool slightly, then put the bowl in the fridge to cool completely

Meanwhile, make the gravy • Peel and finely dice the onion • Warm the oil in the small saucepan • Add the onion and a pinch of salt and stir for 4–5 minutes • Add the reserved marinade, the nutritional yeast, onion powder, stout or beer and bay leaf and simmer, for 4–5 minutes • Mix the cornflour and water together to form a slurry then add this to the pan • Simmer for 4–5 minutes to thicken • Season, then transfer half the gravy to a bowl and leave it to cool slightly, then put the bowl in the fridge to cool completely • Put the other half in a jug and set aside • Finely chop the parsley

Mix the filling • Once the gravy and vegetables in the fridge are cool, add the parsley to the mushrooms and carrot and stir in the gravy

Build the bakes • Cut one sheet of puff pastry into quarters • Lay the quarters on a baking sheet • Spoon a quarter of the filling mixture into the centre of each quarter, leaving a 2cm border around the edges • Cut the second pastry sheet into quarters • Brush the borders of the bases with water and lay the pastry lids on top • Gently crimp around the edges with a fork to seal • Cut 2 slits in the top of each bake • Combine the oat milk and brown sugar and stir until the sugar dissolves • Brush the bakes with the mixture • Bake for 25–30 minutes, until golden

Serve • Warm the remaining gravy • Plate up the bakes, pour over the gravy and serve immediately

MUSHROOM STROGANOFF

We make mushroom stroganoff quite regularly but have never included a recipe in a book. We thought it was high time we righted that wrong! This recipe is super simple but ridiculously effective. Deliciously tender mushrooms in a rich, flavour-packed sauce with lovely mild spice. Serve with rice, mashed potatoes or pasta for a superb, warming, comforting meal!

Serves 4

600g mushrooms
3 vegetarian sausages,
    defrosted if frozen
3 tbsp light olive oil
½ tsp ground black
    pepper
¾ tsp dried thyme
    or the leaves from
    2 fresh sprigs
½–1 tsp paprika
    (optional)
a few dashes of
    Henderson's relish or
    vegan Worcestershire
    sauce (optional)
200g basmati rice
600ml boiling water
1 large onion (about 200g)
salt

For the sauce
2–3 tsp Dijon mustard
350ml barista-style
    dairy-free milk
15g rolled oats
1 lemon
small bunch of fresh
    parsley

Large heavy-based casserole or frying pan over a medium-low heat • Medium saucepan with a lid • Power blender

Get the mushrooms going • Thinly slice about half the mushrooms and thickly slice the rest • Chop the veggie sausages into 3cm chunks • Heat 1 tablespoon of the oil in the casserole or frying pan • Add the thinly sliced mushrooms, veggie sausages and a pinch of salt • Cook for 20 minutes, stirring every few minutes • Mix in the pepper, thyme, paprika and Henderson's or Worcestershire sauce, if using • Turn the heat to low and cook for 5 minutes more, until the mushrooms are reduced and quite dry • Transfer to a plate and set aside

Meanwhile, cook the rice • Rinse the rice under cold running water and tip it into the saucepan • Put the pan on the hob, add the boiling water and a pinch of salt, cover and bring to the boil over a high heat • Stir once to loosen, then reduce the heat to a very low simmer • Cover and cook for exactly 12 minutes • Take the pan off the heat and set it to one side, leaving the lid on but with a small gap to let out steam

Make the sauce • Measure the mustard, milk and oats into the blender • Halve the lemon and squeeze in the juice • Blend

Bring the stroganoff together • Trim, halve and slice the onion • Add the rest of the oil to the pan that you cooked the mushrooms in and turn the heat up to medium • Add the onions and cook for about 8 minutes, until softened and just starting to colour • Add the mushrooms, mix well, cover and leave to cook for 5 minutes more, mixing now and again • Reduce the heat to low, add the sauce and the rest of the mushrooms and heat though for 10 minutes

Serve • Season the stroganoff to taste • Spoon the rice into serving bowls and spoon over the stroganoff • Sprinkle with fresh parsley and serve

HENRY'S MUSHROOM & NOOCH RISOTTO

This deliciously creamy and rich mushroom risotto takes nooch to the next level. Nooch (AKA nutritional yeast) is packed full of cheesy umaminess (like Parmesan) and full of goodness. Winner! You don't have to use the dried porcini here, but they definitely offer an extra depth of flavour! If you really want to turn up the mushroom, try making this with our Mushroom Stock on page 234.

Serves 4

15g dried porcini
    (optional)
500g mushrooms
1 onion
1 celery stick
4 garlic cloves
2 tbsp olive oil
4 sprigs fresh rosemary
    and thyme
300g arborio risotto rice
150ml white wine
25g nutritional yeast, plus
    more for sprinkling
1.4 litres vegetable stock
1 tbsp dairy-free butter
1 lemon
dairy-free cheese
    (optional)
8 fresh chives (optional)
salt and black pepper

Kettle boiled · Large deep-sided saucepan · 1 saucepan

Prepare the mushrooms · Put the porcini, if using, in a bowl and cover with boiling water · Leave for 30 minutes to soak · Finely slice the 500g mushrooms

Cook the onions · Trim and finely chop the onion, celery and garlic · Place the large saucepan on a medium heat and add 1 tablespoon of the olive oil · Add the chopped onion and celery and a pinch of salt · Sauté for 5 minutes until softened, stirring regularly

Add the herbs and rice · Set one sprig of rosemary aside, then pick the leaves from the remaining herbs and chop them finely · Finely chop the soaked porcini, if using · Add half the garlic and sauté for 30 seconds, then add the chopped herbs, porcini, rice and a generous pinch of salt and pepper and stir for another minute · Add the white wine and nutritional yeast and stir until all the liquid from the wine has been absorbed

Slowly add the stock · Add about 200ml of the stock and stir well for 3–4 minutes, until all the stock has been absorbed into the rice · Repeat to use up all the stock over about 20–25 minutes, until the rice is cooked but still firm

Meanwhile, cook the mushrooms · Place the second pan on a medium heat and add the remaining oil, mushrooms and chopped garlic, along with a generous pinch of salt and pepper · Add a whole sprig of rosemary and cook the mushrooms for 10 minutes, until dry and all the liquid has evaporated

Finish the risotto · Stir in the dairy-free butter · Halve the lemon and squeeze over the juice · Taste and add more salt, pepper or lemon if needed · Leave to stand for 2 minutes, then divide the risotto between 4 plates and top each with the cooked mushrooms · Finish with a sprinkle of nooch and/or dairy-free cheese, if using, and some fresh chives

IAN'S INDIAN-STYLE SHEPHERD'S PIE

This recipe marries together a traditional British dish with the flavours of the Indian subcontinent and it works so, so well. The daal filling is truly scrumptious and the mashed potato topping has a magnificent mouthfeel. If you love a traditional shepherd's pie, but fancy an Indian-style twist, this dish is perfect for you. Packed with spices, flavours and bags of comfort.

Serves 6–8

300g dried red lentils
500ml water
200ml coconut milk
1 tsp ground turmeric
1 vegetable stock cube
1 large white onion
1 fresh red chilli
4 garlic cloves
thumb-sized piece
    of fresh ginger
15g fresh coriander
2 tbsp vegetable oil
2 tsp ground coriander
2 tsp ground cumin
2 tsp fenugreek seeds
1 tbsp garam marsala
1 x 400g tin
    chopped tomatoes
1 lime
salt and black pepper

For the topping
1.5kg Maris Piper or
    other floury potatoes
2 tsp ground turmeric
80g dairy-free butter
200ml coconut milk
salt and black pepper

Preheat oven to 160°C • 20 x 30cm lasagne dish • Three large saucepans, two of them warming over medium heat

Prepare the lentils • Rinse the lentils under cold water and them tip into one of the saucepans • Add the water, coconut milk, turmeric, and stock cube and stir to mix • Increase the heat and bring to the boil • Reduce the heat and simmer for 20–30 minutes, stirring occasionally, until the lentils are tender • Set aside

Meanwhile, prepare the rest of the filling • Peel, trim and finely dice the onion • Trim and finely slice the chilli • Peel and finely grate the garlic and ginger • Pick the coriander leaves, set them to one side and finely slice the stems • Heat the oil in the second saucepan • Add the onion and a pinch of salt and stir for 5 minutes • Add the chilli, garlic, ginger and coriander stems and stir for 1 minute • Add the ground coriander, cumin, fenugreek and garam marsala and stir for 1 minute • Add the tinned tomatoes, stir and simmer for 5 minutes • Add the lentils, stir and simmer for 5 minutes • Halve the lime and squeeze over the juice, stir, taste and season • Take the pan off the heat

Make the topping • Peel and quarter the potatoes and put them into the third saucepan • Cover with cold water • Add a big pinch of salt and the turmeric • Place over a high heat and bring to the boil • Cook for 15–17 minutes, until tender and totally cooked through • Drain and leave to steam dry for a couple of minutes, then tip the potatoes back into the pan • Add the dairy-free butter and the coconut milk and mash to a smooth mash • Taste and season with salt and pepper • Finely slice the coriander leaves and stir them into the mash

Assemble the pie • Spread a 1cm thick wall of mash around the edges of the lasagne dish (this will prevent the filling from bubbling over the edges) • Spoon the filling into the dish and smooth the top to make sure it's even • Spoon over the remaining mash and smooth the top • Use a fork to score decorative lines over the top of the pie

Cook and serve • Put the pie in the hot oven and bake for 25 minutes • After this time, switch the oven to grill and cook the top of the pie for 3–5 minutes, until golden and crispy • Take the pie out of the oven and let it rest for 5 minutes • Cut into slices and serve immediately

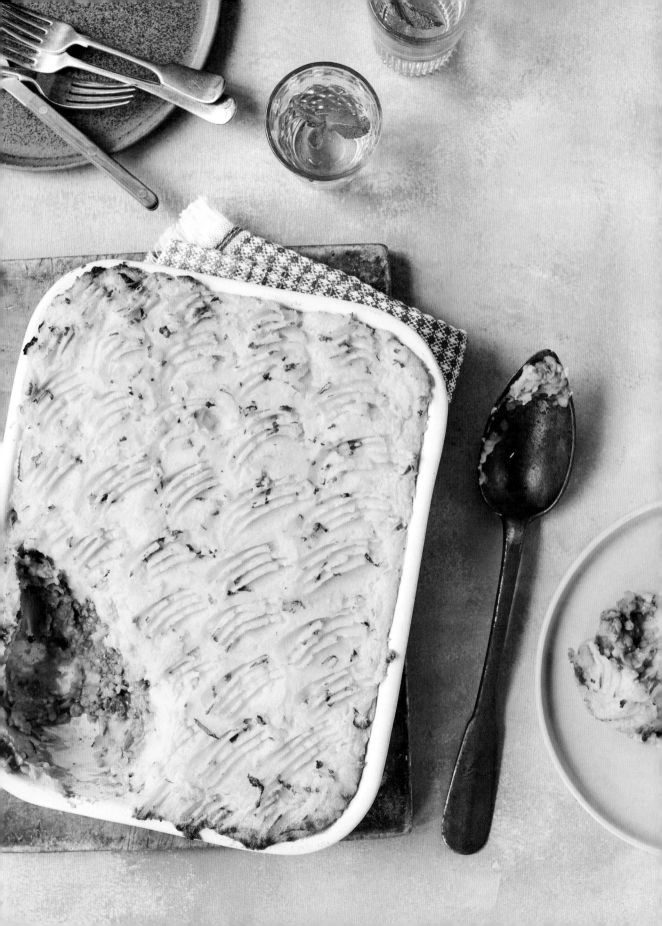

ULTIMATE MOUSSAKA

A wonderful tomato, mushroom and lentil ragu layered up with slices of aubergine and potato, topped with a creamy béchamel and baked until golden and bubbling. This really is the ultimate moussaka! Serve it with a fresh green salad and the smile on your face will be difficult to shift!

Serves 2

3 medium aubergines
(about 900g)
3 large baking potatoes
(about 1kg)
4 tbsp olive oil
salt and black pepper

For the ragu
1 white onion
300g chestnut
mushrooms
3 garlic cloves
2 tsp dried oregano
3 tbsp tomato purée
150g dried puy
or brown lentils
2 x 400g tins
chopped tomatoes
1 vegetable stock cube

For the béchamel
90g hard
dairy-free cheese
1½ tbsp cornflour
600ml dairy-free milk
(oat, almond or soy)
90g dairy-free butter
90g plain flour
1 tsp ground nutmeg
salt and black pepper

To serve
salad

Preheat oven to 180°C • Line 3 baking trays • Large casserole with a lid on a medium-high heat • Small saucepan • Large heatproof bowl

Cook the veg • Trim the aubergines • Slice the aubergine and potatoes into 5mm discs (no need to peel the potatoes!) • Lay out over the lined trays • Drizzle with 3 tablespoons of the olive oil, season with salt and pepper and toss to coat • Cook in the hot oven for 25–30 minutes, until soft.

Meanwhile, make the ragu • Heat the remaining tablespoon of olive oil in the hot casserole • Peel and thinly slice the onion and mushrooms and add to the pan with a big pinch of salt • Fry for 7–10 minutes, stirring occasionally, until soft and starting to turn golden • Peel and grate the garlic into the pan • Add the oregano and tomato purée, stirring to coat • Tip in the lentils and chopped tomatoes, then fill one of the cans with water and add it to the pan along with the stock cube • Bring to the boil, then reduce the heat to a simmer and leave to bubble away for 40–50 minutes, stirring now and then, until the lentils are totally soft and you have a thick ragu, adding a little more water if it looks dry before the lentils are cooked

Make the bechamel • Grate the cheese and put it to one side • In a small bowl, whisk the cornflour with a tablespoon of the milk • Warm the small saucepan over a medium heat • Melt the dairy-free butter, then add the flour and cook, whisking constantly, for 3–4 minutes until the mixture looks dusty, then slowly add the rest of the milk, a little at a time, whisking again to create a smooth sauce • Add the cornflour mixture to the pan, turn up the heat and whisk vigorously until the mixture is thick • Add the ground nutmeg and grated cheese and season generously • Whisk vigorously until the cheese has melted • Set aside

Time to build • Take the ragu off the heat and spoon three-quarters of the mixture into a heatproof bowl • Lay half the potato slices over the ragu in the pan and spoon over a quarter of the remaining ragu, spreading it to the sides • Cover with half the aubergine slices, then another layer of ragu and then the rest of the potato • Spoon over a final layer of ragu and the remaining aubergine slices • Pour the béchamel over the top, spreading it to the edges with the back of a spoon • Return to the oven and bake for 25 minutes • Allow to sit for 10 minutes, then serve up with a big salad

THAI ALL-THE-GREENS CURRY

Laden with green beans, mangetout, broccoli and kale, this might just be the greenest Thai green curry ever! As well as a glorious array of veg, this is full of the deliciously balanced heat, sour and citrus notes that you'd expect. We've gone all out and made the paste from scratch, which we highly recommend you do, too. If you prefer a subtler level of spice, hold some of the paste back and freeze it for another day.

Serves 4

1 medium aubergine
  (about 300g)
50g green beans
50g Tenderstem
  broccoli
50g kale
1 lime
2 tbsp vegetable oil
125g Thai Green Curry
  Paste (shop-bought,
  or use recipe from
  page 238)
1 x 400g tin coconut milk
400ml vegetable stock
1 tbsp soy sauce
1 tbsp sugar
50g mangetout
salt and black pepper

For the rice
200g jasmine rice
pinch of salt
300ml water

For the crispy tofu
140g firm tofu
4 tbsp cornflour
2 tsp salt
oil, for frying

To serve
1 lime
10g fresh coriander
4 tbsp crispy onions

Sieve • Small saucepan with a lid • Tofu press or 2 clean tea towels and a heavy weight • Mixing bowl • Frying pan • Line a plate with kitchen paper • Wok

Cook the rice • Rinse the rice in a sieve under cold water until the water runs clear • Tip into a small saucepan with a pinch of salt and cover with the 300ml of water • Place over a medium-high heat, bring to the boil and then turn the heat right down to a gentle simmer • Cover and leave to cook for 12 minutes • Turn off the heat and leave the rice to steam for a further 10 minutes

Make the crispy tofu • Press the tofu in a tofu press or under a heavy weight for a minimum of 5 minutes • Add the cornflour and salt to the mixing bowl and stir to combine • Cut the tofu into 3cm cubes, tip them into the bowl and toss to coat • Pour the oil into the frying pan until it's 1.5cm deep • Put the pan over a medium heat and heat to 180°C or until the oil sizzles around the edges when you dip in a wooden spoon • Add the tofu cubes to the pan and stir until golden and crispy • Transfer to the plate lined with kitchen paper

Prepare the vegetables • Trim the aubergine and cut it into 2.5cm cubes • Trim and halve the green beans • Trim the broccoli • Stem and shred the kale • Halve the lime

Make the curry • Place the wok over a medium heat and warm the vegetable oil • Add the aubergine, season generously with salt and stir for 1 minute • Add the Thai curry paste and stir for 2 minutes • Add the coconut milk, vegetable stock, soy sauce and sugar and squeeze in the juice of the lime • Turn up the heat, bring to the boil and cook with the lid on for 4–5 minutes • Add the green beans and mangetout, replace the lid and cook for 2–3 minutes • Add the broccoli and cook for 1 minute • Add the kale and cook for a further minute • Taste and season to perfection • Add the tofu to the wok and fold it into the curry

Serve • Cut the remaining lime into wedges • Share the rice between serving bowls and spoon over the curry • Garnish with the fresh coriander and crispy onions and serve immediately with the lime wedges on the side

RED THAI CURRY

Spicier than its green counterpart, red curry is our go-to in any Thai restaurant but make it yourself and it's truly next-level. Here, the heat of the curry is balanced by cherry tomatoes and sweet potatoes, both of which also add an extra hit of red to the mix. Crispy roasted cauliflower florets add a lovely crunch and perfectly cooked jasmine rice is the perfect accompaniment to soak up the fragrant sauce.

Serves 4

2 large sweet potatoes
1 small cauliflower
2 red peppers
1 lime
2 tbsp vegetable oil
125g Thai Red Curry Paste
    (see page 238)
1 x 400ml tin
    coconut milk
400ml low-sodium
    vegetable stock
2 tbsp soy sauce
1 tbsp sugar
200g cherry tomatoes

For the rice

200g jasmine rice
pinch of salt
300ml water

To serve

small bunch of fresh
    coriander
1 lime

Preheat the oven to 180°C • Baking tray • Wok or large frying pan with a lid over a medium heat • Saucepan

Prepare the ingredients • Peel the sweet potatoes and cut them into 3cm chunks • Trim the cauliflower and separate the florets, putting the young leaves to one side (discard the tough outer leaves) • Trim and finely slice the red peppers • Cut one lime in half and the other into wedges • Pick the coriander leaves

Cook the curry • Add 1 tablespoon of the vegetable oil to the wok • Add the peppers and stir for 2 minutes • Add the Thai red curry paste and stir for 2 minutes • Add the sweet potato chunks and stir to coat • Add the coconut milk, vegetable stock, 1 tbsp of soy sauce and the sugar, bring to the boil and simmer for 10–12 minutes • Add the cauliflower florets, cover the pan and simmer for 10 minutes

Meanwhile, cook the rice • Rinse the rice until the water runs clear • Tip into the small saucepan, add a pinch of salt and cover with the water • Bring to the boil then turn the heat right down to a gentle simmer • Cover and leave to cook for 12 minutes • Turn the heat off and leave the rice to steam for a further 10 minutes

Make the crispy cauliflower leaves • Chop any large leaves and lay them on the baking tray • Drizzle over the remaining tablespoon of vegetable oil and the remaining soy sauce • Toss to coat • Put the tray in the hot oven and roast the leaves for 8–10 minutes, until cooked and crisp

Finish the curry • Add the cherry tomatoes to the wok and squeeze in the juice of the lime • Stir to combine and simmer for another 2–3 minutes

Serve • Divide the rice between serving bowls • Spoon over the curry • Dress with the crispy cauliflower leaves • Garnish with the fresh coriander leaves and serve with the lime wedges on the side

HUMMUS PASTA

Hummus pasta is a bit of a BOSH! classic, the video we posted on social media got millions and millions of views. We've cooked hummus pasta for dinner at home a lot over the past couple of years, so we decided to refresh and improve the recipe and include it in this book. Hope you love it as much as we do.

Serves 4

400g spaghetti
    or linguine
10 sun-dried tomatoes,
    plus 2 tsp oil from
    the jar
1 medium red onion
1 garlic clove
10g fresh basil leaves
salt and black pepper

For the Hummus
1 x 400g tin chickpeas
1 garlic clove
1 lemon
3 tbsp tahini
60ml olive oil
50ml water
salt and black pepper

To Serve
simple green salad (we
    like rocket)

Power blender or food processor • Large saucepan of boiling salted water • Frying pan

Make the Hummus • Drain the chickpeas • Peel the garlic • Halve the lemon • Add the chickpeas, garlic, tahini, olive oil and some salt and pepper to the blender or food processor and squeeze over the lemon juice • Blend until very smooth • Add the water and blend again to make a smooth purée (you may need more or less water to get the right consistency)

Prepare the pasta • Add the pasta to the pan of boiling water and cook according to package instructions, until al dente • Reserve the pasta water

Meanwhile, prepare the sauce • Finely slice the sun-dried tomatoes • Peel and finely slice the red onion • Peel and grate the garlic • Place the frying pan over a medium heat and add the sun-dried tomato oil from the jar • Add the red onion and a pinch of salt to the pan and stir for 3 minutes • Add the sun-dried tomatoes and garlic and stir for 2 minutes • Transfer the cooked pasta to the pan along with 2 ladlefuls or about a cup of the pasta water • Carefully toss to combine • Taste and season with salt and pepper

Finish the sauce • Spoon over the hummus and stir it through the pasta, adding a splash more pasta water if necessary to get a really creamy consistency • Taste and season

Serve up • Sprinkle over the basil leaves and some freshly ground pepper and serve immediately with a little green salad on the side

CHEEKY CHOW MEIN

Sometimes, when you're in the mood for a takeaway all you really need is a cheeky chow mein. Well, my friends, here it is! This is the kind of quick, tasty, easy-win meal that makes mid-week cooking a doddle. Crunchy stir-fried veg and wonderfully slippery noodles all dressed in a sweet, sticky sauce that can be thrown together in no time at all. Such a winning dish!

Serves 4

2 garlic cloves
2 fresh red chillies
3cm piece fresh ginger
200g mushrooms
2 large carrots
200g green beans
200g dried
    wholewheat noodles
2 tbsp sesame oil
2 large handfuls of
    beansprouts
sesame seeds,
    for sprinkling

For the sauce
100ml water
6 tbsp hoisin sauce
3 tbsp soy sauce
2 tbsp rice wine vinegar
    or white wine vinegar
2 tbsp sesame oil
1 tbsp sriracha
2 tsp cornflour

Large saucepan of salted water on a high heat • Wok over a high heat

Make the sauce • Measure all the sauce ingredients into a bowl • Whisk to combine • Set aside

Prep the veg • Peel and finely chop the garlic • Trim and finely chop one of the chillies and slice the other • Peel and finely grate the ginger • Finely slice the mushrooms • Peel the carrots and cut them into matchsticks • Cut the green beans into 3cm lengths

Cook the noodles • Add the noodles to the boiling water and cook them according to the packet instructions • Drain and tip into a bowl with 1 tablespoon of the sesame oil to stop them sticking together

Stir-fry the veg • Heat the remaining tablespoon of sesame oil in the hot wok • Add the mushrooms and fry for 5–10 minutes until soft • Add the garlic, chopped chilli and the ginger • Fry for 1 minute • Add the carrots and green beans and toss well • Fry for a few minutes longer • Pour over the sauce and tip in the noodles and beansprouts • Keep tossing, cooking for a couple of minutes until the vegetables are cooked, beansprouts softened a little and the sauce is mixed in

Serve • Tip the chow mein into bowls • Sprinkle with the sesame seeds and the sliced chilli and serve immediately

SWEET

APPLE TARTE TATIN

This classic, indulgent French dessert is named after the Tatin sisters and the hotel in which they invented it. This is the kind of dessert you'd expect to find in a really posh restaurant, but our version is both delicious and really pocket-friendly, especially if you're buying the apples in season. There's a fair bit of prep but it's so, so worth it. Rich, sweet, flaky and beautiful, it's the perfect thing to make if you're looking to turn a few heads and elicit gasps of admiration.

Serves 6

7–8 Pink Lady or
    other firm, sweet
    apples (about 850g)
50g dairy-free butter
    (from a block)
50g caster sugar
320g sheet ready-rolled
    dairy-free puff pastry

For the caramel sauce
100g demerara sugar
50ml water
160g barista-style oat
    milk, at room temp

To serve
dairy-free vanilla
    ice cream

Preheat the oven to 80°C · Baking tray · 20cm ovenproof frying pan with a lid · Small saucepan with a lid

Prepare the apples · Peel the apples · Cut them into quarters and cut out the core · Round off any sharp edges · Place on the baking tray, put the tray in the oven and leave to dry out for 3 hours

Make the caramel base · Preheat the oven to 180°C · Cut the butter into 2cm cubes and dot them evenly around the frying pan · Place the pan over a medium heat and sprinkle over the caster sugar · Gently shake the pan until the butter has melted and the sugar has dissolved · Reduce the heat to low

Cook the apples · Neatly pack the apple quarters into the pan, making a circular pattern around the edges first before filling in the middle · Leave to cook for 5 minutes while you prepare the pastry

Top with the pastry · Unroll the pastry sheet · Place the pan lid on the pastry and cut a circle around it that is 1cm larger than the rim of the pan · Lay the pastry over the apples and tuck the excess down the sides of the pan using a teaspoon · Cut 2 holes in the top to let out steam

Bake the tart · Turn the heat up to medium and cook for 5 minutes, until the butter and sugar is gently bubbling up around the edges of the pan · Transfer the pan to the hot oven and bake for 30 minutes, then reduce the heat to 150°C and bake for a further 25 minutes

Meanwhile, make the caramel sauce · Measure the demerara sugar and water into the small saucepan and stir until the sugar has dissolved · Cover the pan and place it over a medium heat · Leave to bubble for 5 minutes · Remove the lid and cook for a further 4 minutes, without stirring, until the colour has darkened · Take the pan off the heat and leave to rest for 1 minute · Slowly add the milk, whisking continuously to make a very loose sauce · Put the pan back over a high heat and let the sauce reduce for 7–8 minutes, without whisking, until dark and glossy

Serve · Remove the pan from the oven (remember the handle will be hot!) · Place an upturned plate over the pan and carefully flip the tart on to it · Drizzle over a quarter of the sauce · Cut into slices and serve immediately with dairy-free vanilla ice cream and more of the caramel sauce on the side

CHOCOLATE TRAYCAKE

Sometimes, you want to wish a happy birthday without the rigmarole of a full-on cake. This traybake is super quick and easy so there's nothing to stop you bringing smiles of joy to the lucky person. After all, everybody deserves a delicious cake to mark their special day. This one, baked and iced in a single pan, is the perfect way to celebrate. It's sweet, chocolatey and really easy to make, just make sure you get the right number of candles! And have a fire extinguisher nearby just in case.

Serves 18

200g plain flour
250g dark brown sugar
1½ tsp bicarbonate
    of soda
½ tsp baking powder
¼ tsp salt
175ml hot water
90g cocoa powder
200ml oat milk
90ml vegetable oil
2 tsp vanilla extract
1 tbsp white wine vinegar
    or lemon juice

For the icing
100g dark chocolate,
    plus a little extra
    for shaving
400g icing sugar
200g dairy-free butter,
    at room temp
6 tbsp cocoa powder
vegan sprinkles

Preheat the oven to 150°C · **Line a 30 x 20cm ovenproof dish with parchment paper** · **Stand mixer or electric hand-held beaters**

Make the sponge · Measure the flour, sugar, bicarbonate of soda, baking powder and salt into a bowl and whisk to mix · In a separate bowl, combine the hot water and cocoa powder · Whisk together, then add the oat milk, oil, vanilla extract and white wine vinegar or lemon juice · Pour the wet ingredients into the flour mixture and whisk until you have a smooth batter · Tip the mixture into the prepared dish · Transfer to the oven and bake for 20–25 minutes, until risen, cooked through and firm to the touch · Set aside to cool completely

Make the icing · Break the chocolate into pieces and microwave in 15-second bursts until melted · Set aside to cool completely · Sieve the icing sugar into the mixer or a bowl · Add the dairy-free butter and whisk until light and fluffy · Add the cocoa powder and melted chocolate and whisk until smooth

Decorate the cake · Spread the icing evenly over the cake · Top with vegan sprinkles and shavings of dark chocolate

CRUNCHY HONEYCOMB BARS

This is an ode to one of our favourite old-school chocolate snacks, the Crunchie! Golden honeycomb is a lot of fun to make and much easier than you might think. Patience and timing is the key to getting it just right, so make sure you keep your eye on the ball! We found silicone ice-cube trays the best recipients for these sweet treats. They're super cheap and you can pick them up online really easily. Do be careful to leave the honeycomb alone once you've poured it in: don't move it! Leave it to cool in the trays for a perfect shape.

Makes 20–25

200g caster sugar
80g golden syrup
2 tsp bicarbonate of soda
300g dark chocolate
oil, for greasing

To store
a handful of raw rice
   (any kind)

Grease the holes of 2 chunky silicone ice-cube trays and set them tightly together on a cooling rack near the hobs • Medium deep-sided saucepan (about 18cm) on a low heat • Silicone spatula or wooden spoon • Sugar thermometer (optional) • Fine sieve or tea strainer • Balloon whisk • Medium heatproof bowl • Parchment paper • Airtight container for storing

Heat the caramel • Pour the sugar and syrup into the warm saucepan • Stir regularly with a silicone spatula until the sugar has dissolved (about 5–7 minutes) • Once the liquid is clear, turn up the heat to medium-high and bring to a fast boil for 2–3 minutes until it reaches 140°C or you can smell an aroma of warm caramel (it's important not to let the liquid burn, which can happen quickly, so keep a keen eye on it)

Make the honeycomb • Working quickly, take the pan off the heat • Sieve the bicarbonate of soda into the pan and beat with a whisk to combine • When the honeycomb becomes cloudy and bubbles, carefully pour the mixture into the ice cube trays using the silicone spatula to scrape the mixture (it will look uneven and messy but don't touch it or try to press it into the holes as this will alter the texture) • Leave for 30 minutes to solidify

Make the coating • Add 4cm water to the same pan (you don't need to wash the pan – this stage will help to clean it) • Put the pan over a high heat and bring to the boil • Break the chocolate into the heatproof bowl, put the bowl over the pan and stir until melted • Take off the heat and set to one side

Finish the Crunchy Honeycomb Bars • Carefully pop the honeycomb from the trays • Dip the bites in the bowl of melted chocolate, one at a time • Remove with a fork, allowing the excess chocolate to drip back into the bowl • Transfer to parchment paper and leave to set for 1 hour

Store your bars • Place the dry rice in a large container and lay the Crunchy Honeycomb Bars on top, still on their parchment paper so the rice doesn't touch the chocolate (the rice will help absorb any excess moisture and prevent the honeycomb from getting sticky)

NEIL'S TIGER BARS

As kids, we really enjoyed the occasional naughty chocolate bar and we were both big fans of Lion bars, so we decided to have a bash at making our own version, naming our bars after that other famous big cat. Ian's dad Neil is a lifelong Hull City fan. Hull City's nickname is The Tigers, so we felt it was only right to dedicate these bars to him and his beloved football club!

Makes 8

16 ice cream cones
(about 75g)
320g biscuit butter
(Biscoff spread or our
recipe from page 226)

For the butterscotch
130g caster sugar
160g oat milk
130g dairy-free butter
from a block

For the chocolate coating
320g dark chocolate
40g puffed rice cereal

Mixing bowl • Lined baking tray • Large heatproof bowl • Small saucepan

Make the biscuit centre • Blitz 16 ice cream cones in the food processor • Place the blitzed ice cream cones into a large mixing bowl and stir in the biscoff biscuit butter • Line a baking sheet that will fit in your fridge • Use your fingers to form the mixture into 8 equal-sized bars • Place on the baking paper and place them in the fridge to cool until chilled

Meanwhile, make the butterscotch • Warm the sugar in a small pan over a medium high heat making sure you keep your eye on it • As soon as the sugar starts to melt around the edges, reduce the heat and gently shake the pan until all the sugar has melted to a caramel, this should take 3-4 minutes • Take the pan off the heat and continue to shake gently for 1 minute • Put the pan back on the stove and slowly add the oat milk (be very careful as the caramel may spit and froth) • Stir the mixture with a silicone spatula for 5-7 minutes until most of the liquid has evaporated • Add the vegan butter to the pan and fold it into the mixture • Keep stirring the mixture for 5-7 minutes until the butterscotch has thickened considerably and is a golden creamy colour • Transfer the butterscotch to a bowl and leave to set for 2 minutes • Remove the baking tray from the fridge and use two spoons to top the biscuit bars with the butterscotch (be patient here as the butterscotch will be quite sticky) • Place the baking tray back in the fridge to let the butterscotch set • If you have any butterscotch left in the bowl, transfer it to a piece of kitchen paper, allow it to set and cut it into chunks for tasty homemade sweeties!

Make the chocolate topping • Add some boiling water to the caramel pan and bring to a boil • Set a large heatproof bowl over the pan to make a bain marie • Add the chocolate and stir until the chocolate has melted • Take the bowl off the pan and set it down on a clean tea towel • Add the puffed rice cereal and stir it into the chocolate • Leave the chocolate coating to rest for 4-5 minutes

Finish the Tiger Bars • Remove the bars from the fridge, carefully spoon the chocolate coating over the top of the bars and smooth it out with the back of a spoon so the bars have a nice even coating • Put the tray in the fridge, once the bars are chilled, they're ready to eat!

RIGHT GOOD RICE PUD

Over the years, rice pudding has developed a reputation for being an old-fashioned, bland dessert. We thought it deserved a second chance, so we decided to give it the BOSH! treatment. This rice pudding is silky, creamy and downright heavenly. We love it so much that we've given you a core recipe and three additional topping options to try. Whether you go for Bakewell Tart, Banoffee Biscoff or Salted Caramel Apple, you're in for a treat. If you're serving four people, just make one batch of the pudding and one of the toppings.

Serves 4

20g dairy-free butter
4 cardamom pods
3 cloves
100g shortgrain
  white rice
½ orange
50g caster sugar
1 x 400g tin full-fat
  coconut milk
400ml dairy-free milk
1 tsp vanilla extract
1 x topping of your choice
  (see opposite)

Preheat the oven to 130° • **Large ovenproof frying pan with a lid over a low heat**

Prepare the rice pudding • Melt the butter in the ovenproof frying pan • Smash the cardamom pods and scrape the seeds into the pan along with the cloves • Add the rice and stir to coat it in the butter • Zest the orange half and add it to the pan then squeeze in the juice • Add the sugar and stir • Add the coconut milk, dairy-free milk and vanilla • Stir and bring to a simmer • Cover and transfer the pan to the oven to bake for 30 minutes • Remove the lid, stir well and return to the oven, uncovered, to bake for another 30 minutes, until cooked through (if it looks too dry, stir in a splash more milk) • Place back in the oven for another 10 minutes while you prepare the toppings

Serve • Stir the rice pudding and spoon it into small bowls • Add your favourite topping and serve

BAKEWELL TART

Makes enough for 4 portions
of rice pudding

2 tbsp flaked almonds
2 tbsp raspberry jam
1 tsp icing sugar

Small frying pan

Set the small frying pan over
a low heat • Tip the almonds
into the pan and cook for
3–5 minutes, stirring regularly
• Spoon the jam on to the rice
pudding and sprinkle with the
toasted almond flakes • Dust
with the icing sugar and serve

BANOFFEE BISCOFF

Makes enough for 4 portions
of rice pudding

1 tbsp dairy-free butter
2 bananas
2 tbsp dark brown sugar
a squeeze orange juice
4 Biscoff biscuits

Small frying pan

Place the small frying pan
over a medium heat and melt
the butter • Slice the bananas
and add them to the pan
along with the sugar • Let it
gently caramelise for about
5 minutes • Squeeze in the
orange juice and leave for
another minute, then tip the
mixture over the rice pudding
• Crush the biscuits and
sprinkle them over the top
before serving

SALTED CARAMEL APPLE

Makes enough for 4 portions
of rice pudding

1 tbsp dairy-free butter
1 apple
1 tbsp dark brown sugar
½ tsp fine salt
pinch of sea salt

Small frying pan

Place the small frying pan
over a low heat and melt
the butter • Core and slice
the apple and add it to the
pan along with the sugar and
½ teaspoon of fine salt • Let
the apples gently caramelise
for 8–10 minutes, moving
them around gently every
now and then to stop them
catching • Once the apples
are sticky and dark brown, tip
them over the rice pudding
and sprinkle over a few sea
salt flakes before serving

FRYING PAN BISCOFF BROWNIE

This blinder of a recipe is the sequel to our frying pan cookie in *Speedy BOSH!* Crisp and chewy round the outside, soft and gooey in the middle, packed with indulgent chocolatey deliciousness, this is the quintessential brownie, but laced with Biscoff or, even better, our BOSHcoff recipe (see page 226) and studded with caramelised hazelnuts to make it that extra bit special.

Serves 8

300g unpeeled potatoes
100ml water
200g caster sugar
60g cocoa powder
100g dark chocolate
150g sunflower oil, plus
    extra for greasing
¾ tsp apple
    cider vinegar
a pinch of salt
110g plain flour
1 tsp baking powder
175g Biscoff spread

For the candied hazelnuts
75g blanched hazelnuts
50g caster sugar
25ml water
½ tsp sea salt
    flakes (optional)

Preheat the oven to 170°C · Baking tray · Set a steamer or metal colander over a small saucepan with 3–5cm water over a medium-high heat · Grease a medium ovenproof frying pan with oil · Rubber spatula · Grease a baking tray or sheet of parchment paper with plenty of oil · Food processor

Steam the potatoes · Put the potatoes in the steamer or colander, cover and steam for 30–40 minutes, until tender · Set aside to cool just slightly

Meanwhile, candy the hazelnuts · Spread the nuts over the baking tray · Put the tray in the oven for 5–10 minutes, until the nuts are lightly toasted · Put the sugar and water into the greased frying pan and set the pan over a medium–high heat · As soon as the liquid starts to bubble, reduce the heat to medium · Add the toasted nuts, mix well with a rubber spatula and let it bubble away, tilting the pan now and then, until the water evaporates and you have a light golden syrup that coats the nuts (about 5 minutes) · Quickly scrape the nuts on to the greased baking tray or parchment paper · Sprinkle over the salt and leave to cool

Meanwhile, prep the chocolate · Wash out the small saucepan and add the water, sugar, cocoa powder and chocolate · Mix well · Set the pan over a low heat, folding the mixture with a rubber spatula now and again · Once melted, stir until smooth and take off the heat · Scrape into a bowl and set aside to cool until just warm

Make the brownie mixture · Once they're cool enough to handle but still hot, peel and chop the potatoes into the food processor · Blitz until smooth · Add the oil in a slow and steady stream until combined · Add the vinegar and salt and pulse to mix · Tip into the bowl with the chocolate mixture · Fold until just mixed · Add the flour and baking powder to a separate bowl and mix to combine, then sieve the flours over the chocolate mixture and fold together without overmixing · Scrape into the greased frying pan · Spread the Biscoff evenly over the top

Bake the brownie · Put the pan in the hot oven and bake for 17–20 minutes · Sprinkle over the candied hazelnuts and either leave to stand for 10 minutes before digging in while it's hot, or leave to cool, cut into slices and serve

CHOCOLATE GANACHE POTS

These silky, rich and decadent chocolate ganache pots make the perfect end to a romantic meal, though to be honest they're so good that you might want to bin the date and stay home alone. However you're eating them, they need a good few hours setting time in the fridge, so they're perfect for making ahead and serving straight from the fridge.

Makes 6

1 x 400g tin full-fat
   coconut milk
150g dairy-free dark
   chocolate
2 tbsp good-quality
   cocoa powder
1 tsp vanilla extract
2 tbsp caster sugar
1 tsp sea salt, plus extra
   for sprinkling

Small saucepan over a low heat • 6 small glasses or jars

Make the chocolate pots • Pour the coconut milk into the pan and warm gently until just simmering • Roughly chop the chocolate and add it to the hot milk • Whisk until completely melted • Take the pan off the heat and add the cocoa, vanilla, sugar and a teaspoon of salt • Whisk again until totally smooth • Pour into glasses or jars • Leave to cool for 30 minutes, then cover and put in the fridge for a minimum of 4 hours or overnight

Serve • Take the pots out of the fridge, sprinkle over some sea salt flakes, grab some teaspoons and tuck in

SALTED CARAMEL STICKY TOFFEE PUDDING

If you were to poll the population of the UK on their favourite dessert, we'd bet good money that Sticky Toffee Pudding would come out on top, and at BOSH! HQ we're no different! It's the kind of proper hug-in-a-bowl pudding that perfectly finishes off a lazy meal on a Sunday afternoon. In this version, sticky dates impart a delicious caramel flavour to the fluffy sponge, which floats atop a bubbling sea of toffee. We've suggested serving it with dairy-free ice cream, but vegan custard would also work a treat.

Serves 8–10

250g dates
300ml oat milk
2 tbsp ground linseeds
175g self-raising flour
1 tsp bicarbonate of soda
175g dark brown sugar
200ml vegetable oil

For the sauce
250g dark brown sugar
250g dairy-free cream
200ml water
1–2 tsp salt

To serve
dairy-free ice cream

Preheat the oven to 160°C • 20 x 30cm ovenproof dish • Medium saucepan on a medium-low heat • Blender or food processor

Prepare the sponge ingredients • Stone the dates and put them in the saucepan • Add the oat milk and linseeds • Gently warm for 3–5 minutes until thickened and the dates are soft • Measure the flour, bicarbonate of soda and sugar into a bowl and mix, breaking up any sugar lumps • Leave the date and oat milk mixture to cool slightly, then transfer to the blender or food processor and blend to make a smooth sauce • Add the oil and blitz again • Set aside

Make the sauce • Measure the ingredients for the sauce into a medium saucepan • Set the pan over a low heat and leave for 5 minutes, stirring occasionally, until the sugar has dissolved

Bake the pudding • Tip the date mixture into the flour, whisking well to remove any lumps • Spread the batter over the base of the baking dish • To help spread the sauce over the batter, invert a dessert spoon over it and pour the hot sauce over the back of a spoon (don't worry about it being a little messy!) • Bake for 25–30 minutes, until the sponge is soft to the touch and wobbles slightly when you shake the pan

Serve • Spoon the pudding into bowls • Serve with big scoops of dairy-free ice cream

BOSH! GINGERBREAD PEOPLE

A lot of gingery treats have a snappy crunch to them but with this recipe we wanted to recreate the kind of gingerbread you get at a local bakery, which has got a slightly softer, bendier texture. It took a while to perfect this recipe, but we got there eventually! If you're like us and you love gingerbread, we urge you to give it a try.

Makes 12

350g plain flour
½ tsp salt
150g light brown sugar
1 tsp bicarbonate of soda
1 tsp xanthan gum
6 cloves or ½ tsp
   ground cloves
¼ tsp ground nutmeg
3½ tsp ground ginger
1 tsp ground cinnamon
100g dairy-free butter,
   cold from the fridge
1 tsp apple cider vinegar
50ml golden syrup
80ml dairy-free milk

For the icing
150g icing sugar
vegan sprinkles (optional)

Preheat the oven to 160°C fan • Lightly dust 2 large baking sheets with flour • Lightly dust a clean work surface and a large sheet of parchment paper with flour • Cookie cutters in the shape of people • Piping bag fitted with a fine drawing nozzle (or a piping bag you can snip the end off)

Make the dough • Put the flour, salt, sugar, bicarbonate of soda and xanthan gum into the bowl • Grind the cloves if you're using whole spices and add them to the mix • Grate in the nutmeg • Add the rest of the spices and stir to mix • Cut the dairy-free butter into cubes and rub it into the flour mixture until you have a texture like fine breadcrumbs • In a separate bowl or jug, mix together the vinegar, syrup and dairy-free milk until smooth • Make a well in the centre of the dry ingredients • Pour in the wet mixture and mix thoroughly with a butter knife • Tip on to the work surface and shape into a ball

Cut out the shapes and bake • Roll out the dough to 1cm thick on the sheet of parchment paper • Cut out the shapes with the cookie cutters • Transfer the gingerbread people to the prepared baking sheets, leaving 2cm between them so they don't stick together • Put the trays in the oven and bake for 10–15 minutes, until lightly golden • Remove and leave to cool on the trays

Make the icing • Measure the icing sugar into a bowl • Add water, a few drops at a time, mixing with a spoon until it starts to make a fairly firm but pipeable paste • Spoon the icing into the piping bag

Decorate your gingerbread people • Snip a tiny bit off the end of the piping bag or use the fine nozzle to pipe clothes and faces on to your characters, then decorate with sprinkles, if using • Leave to set before serving

LEMON DRIZZLE TRAYCAKE

Lemon drizzle is probably Britain's favourite cake – so popular, in fact, that we made our own lemon cakes, which you can buy in shops! It's so great when you make it yourself, so here it gets a facelift in traybake form, making it easy to slice into bars and share with friends. We've taken the drizzle one step further and topped the cake with a beautifully feathered combo of classic white lemon icing and vibrant lemon curd. When life gives you lemons, make cake. And make a beautiful cake, like this one.

Serves 12

2 lemons
275g self-raising flour
200g caster sugar
1 tsp baking powder
100ml oat milk
120ml vegetable
   or sunflower oil
70ml water

For the lemon curd
2 tsp cornflour
60ml oat milk
60g sugar
¼ tsp turmeric

For the icing
200g icing sugar
1 tbsp cold water

Preheat the oven to 160°C • Line a 17 x 25cm ovenproof dish with parchment paper • Cooling rack • Small saucepan • Piping bag (optional)

Make the sponge • Zest the 2 lemons and cut them in half • Measure the flour, sugar, baking powder and zest into a bowl and whisk to mix • Squeeze the juice of ½ a lemon into a small bowl • Add the oat milk, mix well and set aside • Pour the oil into the dry mixture • Add the water and the lemon milk • Whisk well, then tip into the tin and spread it out evenly • Transfer to the hot oven and bake for 20–25 minutes, until lightly golden and cooked through • Transfer to a cooling rack and leave to cool completely

Make the lemon curd • Tip the cornflour into the small pan • Add a splash of the oat milk and whisk to combine, then add the rest of the oat milk, whisking to make sure there are no lumps • Squeeze in the juice of one of the lemons, catching the pips in your other hand • Add the sugar and turmeric • Set the pan over a medium heat and whisk until thick, about 5 minutes • Tip into a bowl and set aside to cool

Make the icing • Measure the icing sugar and water into a bowl • Squeeze in the juice of the last lemon half a drop or two at a time • Mix until smooth and the consistency of double cream

Ice the traycake • If you're using a piping bag, spoon the curd into it • Pop the cooled cake back into the oven dish • Pour over the icing and use the back of a spoon or a spatula to spread it over the cake • Working quickly so that the icing doesn't set, rotate the dish 90 degrees • Use a spoon or the piping bag to draw lines of lemon curd about 2–3cm apart • Use the long end of a spoon or a skewer to drag the curd left and right to create a marble effect • Allow the icing to set completely (about 1 hour) • Slice and serve

MISSISSIPPI MUD PIE

'Mrs M, Mrs I, Mrs S, S, I, Mrs S, S, I, Mrs P, P, I.' That's how you spell Mississippi and this recipe is how you make a world-beating vegan Mississippi mud pie. Thick bourbon crust covered with a brownie-like layer of squidgy chocolate pudding and topped with a silky chocolate custard. This one is such a goodie. Enjoy! We've even managed to bake some healthiness into it in the form of a squash. Works an absolute treat, trust us.

Serves 10–12

For the crust
300g bourbon biscuits
100g caster sugar
10g cocoa powder
60ml vegetable oil

For the chocolate custard
700g squash
10ml + 1 tbsp vegetable oil
250ml oat or almond milk
2 tsp vanilla extract
35g cocoa powder
25g plain flour
100g caster sugar

For the pudding layer
125ml dairy-free milk
1 tsp apple cider vinegar
100ml light oil
60g cocoa powder
1 tsp vanilla extract
1 heaped tsp
   instant coffee
150g caster sugar
100g plain flour
1 tsp baking powder
a pinch of salt

To serve
dairy-free cream
   (optional)

Preheat the oven to 180°C · Large roasting tin · Grease a 23cm spring-form cake tin or pie dish · Power blender or food processor and a stick blender · Rubber spatula

Bake the squash · Peel and trim the squash and cut it into 3cm chunks · Tip into the roasting tin and toss with 1 tablespoon oil · Cover with foil, put the tin in the oven and roast for 30 minutes, until tender

Make the crust · Put the biscuits into the blender or food processor and blitz to crumbs · Add the sugar, cocoa powder and oil · Pulse until evenly combined · Scrape the mixture into the tin, using the rubber spatula to press it firmly into the base and bringing the edges 5–6cm up the sides of the tin · Transfer to the oven and bake for 5–6 minutes, until cooked through · Remove from the oven and set aside to cool

Make the pudding layer · Pour the milk and vinegar into a jug and mix to combine · Leave for 5 minutes to curdle slightly · Measure the oil, cocoa, vanilla and coffee into a bowl and mix until smooth · Add the curdled milk and sugar and whisk gently until smooth · Sieve the flour, baking powder and salt into a large bowl · Add the wet mixture and fold everything together using the rubber spatula, being careful not to overmix it · Scrape everything into the tin over the crust and bake for 20 minutes, until springy and with a crust, but gooey and brownie-like in the middle · Remove from the oven and leave to cool in the tin

Make the chocolate custard · Add the cooked squash, a good splash of the milk, the remaining oil, vanilla and cocoa powder to the blender and blend until smooth (you may need to do this in batches) · Pour the remaining milk, flour and sugar into a small saucepan and set it over a low heat · Cook for 1 minute, whisking constantly, to dissolve the sugar · Add the chocolatey squash and mix well · Turn the heat to medium-low and heat for 8–10 minutes, until thickened, mixing all the time until the mixture has reduced by 10 per cent · Leave to cool slightly, then pour over the brownie layer in the tin, smoothing the top with a spatula

Set the pie · Leave the pie to cool to room temperature, then place it in the fridge and leave it to set for 2–3 hours or preferably overnight

Serve · Take the pie out of the fridge, carefully remove the tin and cut into slices · Serve with a drizzle of dairy-free cream on top, if you like

STAPLES

HOME-MADE TOFU

Part recipe, part science project, making tofu from scratch is fun and surprisingly easy. It's also more cost-effective than buying tofu from a supermarket. And, most importantly, if you do it right you can get a wonderful flavour in your tofu as well as controlling your texture, pressing it for longer to get a firmer tofu. If you're going to try this, which we definitely recommend you do, you'll need a tofu press, which can be picked up online pretty cheaply. Ours (pictured) cost £6, which is pretty reasonable as long as you use it a few times.

Makes 1 large block

400g dried soya beans
4 litres + 3 tbsp
    cold water
2 tsp nigari

Power blender • Very large stock pot or 2 large saucepans with lids • Muslin cloths • Colander • Put the base of your tofu press in a small roasting tin and lay a muslin inside • Pressing weights (such as tins of food) • Small sieve

The night before, prepare the soya beans • Pour the beans into a large bowl, cover with 1 litre of the water and leave to hydrate overnight • Once hydrated and drained the beans should weigh approximately 900g

Prepare the soy milk • Rinse the hydrated beans under cold water • Transfer 180g of the beans to the blender and cover with 600ml of the water • Blend until smooth • Pour the puréed beans into the stock pot • Repeat to blend all the beans

Make the soy milk • Turn the heat on to medium and warm the blended beans for 15–20 minutes, stirring every 30 seconds to make sure the mixture doesn't catch • Use a spoon to gently scoop out any froth that forms • Reduce the heat to low and simmer for a further 5–10 minutes • Drape a muslin cloth over a colander and set it on top of a large mixing bowl or clean saucepan • Strain the mixture through the cloth to catch the pulp • Once it's cooled enough to handle, twist the cloth to squeeze as much liquid into the bowl as you can • The pulp is edible and nutritious, so if you wish to cook with it, look up recipes online • If it is in a bowl, pour the strained milk into a clean stock pot or saucepans with lids

Make the tofu • Add the nigari and 3 tablespoons of water to a tumbler and stir until dissolved • Slowly pour the mixture into the soy milk and stir for 10 seconds • Put the lid on the pan and leave for 15 minutes to curdle and form curds • Use the small sieve to scoop the curd into the prepared tofu press • Once you've removed as much of the curd as you can, neatly fold the muslin cloth over the top of the curds • Put the top of the tofu press in place and gently squeeze down to compress the curds • Place a weight on top and leave for a minimum of 15 minutes (leaving it for 30 minutes will create a firmer texture)

Eat or store the tofu • Remove the tofu from the press and unwrap it • The tofu is now ready to marinate, cook and eat • Alternatively, freeze it in a freezer-safe container or place in a container, cover with water and store in the fridge for up to 5 days

HOME-MADE SPREADS

We get through an awful lot of tasty spreads at BOSH! HQ, so we wanted to give you recipes for home-made options that won't break the bank and are just as good as shop-bought versions (if not better!). We like our peanut butter with a bit of crunch but blitz it to your liking. For the other two recipes, you want them smoooooth so be patient with the food processor to be sure to get them to a nice silky consistency, but be careful not to overheat them by over processing as that can cause them to seize.

To sterilise your jars, set the oven to 140°C. Wash the jars and lids thoroughly in warm soapy water, rinse and transfer straight to the oven to heat for 15 minutes. Leave to cool to room temperature.

NOTELLA

Makes 2 medium jars

300g blanched hazelnuts
175g caster sugar
200g dark chocolate
pinch of salt
1 tsp vanilla extract
125–150ml barista-style oat milk

Preheat the oven to 160°C • Baking tray • Food processor • 2 clean sterilised jam jars (see instructions above)

Roast and blitz the hazelnuts • Spread the hazelnuts out on a baking tray • Put the tray in the oven and roast the nuts for 8–10 minutes, until their aroma has been released and they're a light golden colour • Transfer to a plate and leave to cool to room temperature • Pour the nuts and sugar into the food processor and blitz for 5–6 minutes, scraping down the sides with a spatula every so often

Add the rest of the ingredients • Finely chop the chocolate and put it into a microwavable bowl • Put the bowl in the microwave and melt the chocolate in 30-second bursts • Add the salt and vanilla extract to the food processor and pulse to combine • Add the melted chocolate and pulse again • Turn the processor on and gradually pour in 125ml of the oat milk • Stop the processor, remove the lid and check the consistency – if you think it needs loosening, pulse in the remaining oat milk

Store • Pour the Notella into the sterilised jars and leave to cool to room temperature • Put the lids on, transfer to the fridge and use within 2 weeks

PEANUT BUTTER

Makes 2 medium jars

400g blanched peanuts
1tsp sea salt flakes

**Preheat the oven to 160°C • Baking tray •
Food processor • 2 clean sterilised jam jars
(see instructions 224)**

Roast the peanuts • Spread the peanuts out
on a baking tray • Put the tray in the oven and
roast the nuts for 8–10 minutes, until their
aroma has been released and they're a light
golden colour • Transfer to a plate and leave
to cool to room temperature • Pour the nuts
and sugar into the food processor and blitz
for 5–6 minutes, scraping down the sides with
a spatula every so often

Make the butter • If you want crunchy peanut
butter, pour about a quarter of the roasted
peanuts into the processor and pulse until
roughly chopped • Scrape out the mixture
and set aside • Add the rest of the peanuts
to the processor and blend for 8–10 minutes,
scraping down the sides with a spatula every
so often • Be patient, it will look like the
process isn't working for a good few minutes
– do not add any liquid as this will make the
butter seize • When the peanuts have turned
into peanut butter, add the salt and blitz for
another 10–15 seconds • Stir in the reserved
crunchy peanuts, if using

Store • Scrape into the sterilised jam jars,
put the lids on and store in the cupboard •
Use within 2 weeks

BOSHCOFF SPREAD

Makes 2 medium jars

250g Biscoff biscuits
75g caster sugar
pinch of salt
75ml barista-style oat milk
150ml coconut oil

**Food processor • 2 clean sterilised jam jars
(see instructions 224)**

Blitz the dry ingredients • Break the biscuits
into the food processor and blitz into crumbs
• Add the sugar and salt and pulse to combine

Warm the coconut oil • Put the coconut oil
in a microwavable bowl • Put the bowl in the
microwave and heat in 10 second bursts until
melted

Blend the wet and dry ingredients • Add the
oat milk to the food processor and blend until
smooth • Keep the machine running and add
the oil in a slow and steady stream until the
butter is smooth

Store • Transfer to the sterilised jam jars, put
the lids on and put the jars in the fridge • Use
within 2 weeks

HOME-MADE PASTA

Making your own pasta from scratch is one of those things that is surprisingly easy to do, but will be sure to impress your friends and family no end. There's no need for any specialist kit either … Yes, a pasta machine will come in handy if you're knocking up pappardelle on the regular (you can get them for a fair price), but for the pasta novice a rolling pin and a bit of elbow grease can work too. If you are doing it by hand, do it carefully and take your time! We've got two options for you here, a classic white pasta and a vibrant green version, packed with spinachy goodness. The method is almost identical for both but with the addition of spinach for the green version, so just skip the first step if making the white variety. *Buon appetito!*

Makes 600g white or green pasta

300g fine semolina
150g pasta flour, plus extra for dusting
1 tsp salt
75ml aquafaba (the drained water from about 1 x 400g tin chickpeas)
50–75ml warm water

If you are making green pasta
100g fresh or frozen spinach

To serve
tasty sauce such as one of our pestos (pages 230–231) or Hummus Pasta (page 190)

Food processor • Clean work surface dusted liberally with semolina • Kettle boiled • Rolling pin • Baking tray dusted with semolina • Pastry cutter or pizza wheel • Clean tea towel

If you are making green pasta, prepare the spinach • If you're using fresh spinach, wilt it by pouring boiling water over it or cooking it briefly in a pan of boiling water • Defrost frozen spinach, if using • Press out as much water as you can so that you're left with the cooked spinach leaves

Make the pasta dough • Measure the semolina, flour, salt and aquafaba into the food processor (if you are making green pasta, also add the drained spinach) • Turn it on and slowly add the water until the dough clumps together and pulls away from the sides of the bowl (if it doesn't clump, very slowly add a little more water until it does) • Tip the dough on to the prepared work surface and knead for 3 minutes until you have a smooth ball • Divide into 4 equal pieces, wrap in cling film and put in the fridge for 30 minutes or up to 2 hours

Roll out the dough • Place the rested dough on your well-dusted work surface • Dust your rolling pin with semolina and roll out the dough into a very long, thin strip • Lightly dust it with more semolina and rub the pasta gently with your hands to spread out the semolina and dry out the pasta • Fold each end of the pasta up so that they meet in the middle and turn the pasta 90 degrees • Repeat 3 more times, rolling out the strip and folding up each end to help align the gluten and make a smoother pasta, which should feel smooth and dry to the touch

Shape the pasta • Roll the dough out as long and thin as you can • Cut it into thin strips using a pastry cutter to get wavy edges for mafaldine or a pizza wheel for straight-edged shapes like tagliatelle • Lift the strips at the middle and twist them on to your dusted baking tray in bundles • Cover the bundles with the tea towel until you're ready to cook

Cook your pasta • Fill a large saucepan with boiling water and salt generously • Cook for 2–3 minutes before using tongs to transfer the pasta into whatever sauce you're using

ALL THE PESTO

Packed with flavour, quick to make, easy on the wallet – we LOVE pesto! So much so that we're giving you five incredible recipes for it. The first two are Henry's classic ultimate red and green pestos that were too special not to include. The final three are Ian's fridge-raid pestos that are designed to use up the leftovers and odds and ends from the back of your fridge and give them new life in the form of vibrant, punchy pastes that can be used to dress pasta, top veg or tofu, or to just eat straight from the jar! We've also given you Ian's core fridge-raid pesto formula, so that you can knock up your own tasty pestos from what you already have to hand.

HENRY'S CLASSIC PESTOS

ULTIMATE FIERY CHILLI RED PESTO

Makes 250–300g

1 small garlic clove
160g roasted red peppers from a jar
125g sun-dried tomatoes
½ fresh red chilli (about 5g)
20g ground almonds
20g nutritional yeast
½ tbsp dried chilli flakes
35ml extra-virgin olive oil
salt and black pepper

Food processor or power blender

Prep the ingredients • Peel the garlic and add it to the food processor

Blitz • Add all the other ingredients and pulse until you have a textured pesto • Taste and season to perfection with salt, pepper and more chilli flakes if you like it really spicy!

ULTIMATE GREEN PESTO

Makes 250–300g

2 lemons
60g pine nuts
30g fresh basil
30g fresh parsley
10g nutritional yeast
1 tbsp white miso
90ml extra-virgin olive oil
salt and black pepper

Food processor

Prep the ingredients • Cut the lemons in half and squeeze the juice into the food processor, catching any pips with your spare hand (you will need about 60ml)

Blitz • Add all the remaining ingredients and blitz until you have a lovely textured pesto • Taste and season to perfection with salt, pepper and more lemon, if you like

IAN'S FRIDGE-RAID PESTO FORMULA

Makes 250–300g

2 garlic cloves or 1 tsp
    roasted garlic paste
½ lemon or 1 tsp vinegar
50g mixed herbs and
    vegetables
handful of toasted nuts or
    toasted bread
    (about 40g)
1 tbsp nutritional yeast
100ml olive oil
salt and black pepper

Food processor or power blender

Blitz • Place all the ingredients in the food processor and pulse if you like a chunky pesto or blend for a smoother texture • Season to taste

ROCKET, PARSLEY & HAZELNUT

½ lemon
2 garlic cloves
50g rocket
10g fresh parsley, stems and leaves
handful of toasted hazelnuts
1 tbsp nutritional yeast
100ml extra-virgin olive oil
salt and black pepper

Prep the ingredients • Zest the lemon and squeeze the juice into the food processor

Blitz • Place all the ingredients in the food processor and pulse if you like a chunky pesto or blend for a smoother texture • Season to taste

CARROT, FENNEL TOP & ALMOND

½ lemon
2 cloves roasted garlic
60g carrot tops / fennel tops and
    fronds or a mixture of both
handful of toasted almonds, flaked
    or whole
1 tbsp nutritional yeast
100ml olive oil
salt and black pepper

Prep the ingredients • Zest the lemon and squeeze the juice into the food processor

Blitz • Place all the ingredients in the food processor and pulse if you like a chunky pesto or blend for a smoother texture • Season to taste

COURGETTE, ALMOND & MINT

1 small or ½ medium courgette
½ lemon
2 handfuls of fresh mint leaves
handful of fresh basil
handful of toasted almonds, flaked
    or whole
1 tbsp nutritional yeast
100ml olive oil
salt and black pepper

Prep the ingredients • Place the courgette directly on a cooker flame or in a hot griddle pan and leave for 10–15 minutes, turning occasionally, to blacken on all sides • Roughly chop and add to the food processor • Zest the lemon and squeeze in the juice

Blitz • Place all the ingredients in the food processor and pulse if you like a chunky pesto or blend for a smoother texture • Season to taste

CHILLI & GARLIC NAAN

These chilli garlic naan are a must with any BOSH! curry feast. Soft, pillowy and laden with aromatic garlic and chilli, they're just the thing for scooping up delicious curry. Just make sure you cook them quickly so the little flecks of chilli are cooked but not burnt.

Makes 4

250g strong white bread flour, plus extra for dusting
1 x 7g sachet dried fast-action yeast
1 tsp salt
1 tsp sugar
100g dairy-free yoghurt
70ml water (or more if needed)

For the chilli garlic mix
6 fresh green chillies
3 large cloves garlic
pinch of chilli flakes
1 tsp salt
3 tbsp oil

First, make the naan • Put all the naan ingredients into a bowl and mix well, kneading between your fingers until the ingredients come together to form a uniform dough • Add a touch more water to loosen, if it feels too dry • Dust some flour over a clean surface and knead the dough firmly for 7 minutes, punching, flattening, folding then rotating 90 degrees, then repeating • The dough will firm up and become more springy • Use your hands to form a nice round ball, then place in a lightly oiled bowl, cover and rest in a warm place for 90 minutes, until the dough has roughly doubled in size

Make the mix • Finely chop your chillies and garlic, then add to a small bowl with the chilli flakes, salt and oil • Mix well.

Prepare the dough • Place the dough on a floured surface and knead by hand for 2-3 minutes more, then form into a ball and use a knife to cut into quarters • Roll each piece of dough into an oval shape that's about 30cm long (no longer than the width of your saucepan!) • Spoon a quarter of the chilli mix over a naan, then use the rolling pin to gently roll them, pressing the chilli and garlic pieces into the surface of the naan.

Cook the naan • Place a frying pan on a high heat and add a good splash of vegetable oil • Wait until the pan is really quite hot, then place the naan, chilli-side facing up, into the pan • Cook for 2 minutes, by which time some bubbles should have appeared and the bottom should be golden brown • Use a spatula to flip the naan, and cook for a further 60 seconds, until the chillies are still green but slightly browned, and the naan has started to brown too • Remove and place on a chopping board • Quickly rinse the pan to get rid of any remaining chilli pieces, then re-oil the pan and repeat for all the remaining naan

HOME-MADE STOCKS

A great stock is the base of so many dishes and making your own from scratch adds a complexity of flavour that you simply don't get from a stock cube. It's a great waste-saving hack, as you can use a variety of peelings or offcuts that you would otherwise have thrown away. We've given you two delicious versions here, both of which can be paired with any dish that calls for stock in this book.

MUSHROOM STOCK

Makes 1.5 litres

½ onion
250g mushrooms
2 tbsp olive oil
2 star anise
2 whole cloves
1 tbsp nutritional yeast
1 tbsp salt
1 tsp garlic powder
2 tsp Marmite
1 tsp onion granules
2 litres water

Stock pot over a medium heat • Kettle boiled • Clean containers for storage

Prepare the vegetables • Peel the onion and cut it into wedges • Chop the mushrooms

Start the stock • Add the olive oil to the pan • Add the onion and mushrooms to the hot oil • Stir, cover and sweat down the mushrooms for 3–4 minutes.

Add the rest of the ingredients • Add all the remaining ingredients and bring to the boil • Lower the heat, cover and simmer for 30 minutes until dark and rich

Store the stock • Strain the stock through a sieve and cool to room temperature • Transfer to freezer-safe containers and freeze until needed, or store in the fridge for up to 5 days

ULTIMATE VEG STOCK

Makes 1.5 litres

3 leek tops
1 large celery root
1 large fennel root
1 large parsnip or carrot
1 tbsp olive oil
1½ tbsp fennel seeds
1½ tbsp peppercorns
1½ tbsp salt
6 bay leaves
5 thyme sprigs
2 rosemary sprig
2 sage sprig
2 litres water

Stock pot • Clean containers for storage

Prepare the vegetables • Roughly chop the leek tops and root vegetables

Cook the stock • Place the pot over a medium heat and add the olive oil • Add the chopped vegetables and stir for 2 minutes until they start to soften • Add the fennel seeds, peppercorns and salt and stir for 1 minute • Add the remaining ingredients and bring to the boil • Lower the heat and simmer for 30 minutes until the stock has reduced and darkened

Finish and store • Taste and adjust the seasoning if necessary • Strain the stock through a sieve into a jug and leave to cool to room temperature • Transfer to freezer-safe containers or ice-cube trays and freeze until needed, or store in the fridge and use within 5 days

HENRY'S CURRY STOCK

From toasting your spices to long, low simmers, building a delicious curry from the ground up is a labour of love that can't be rushed. Or can it? Make a big batch of this deliciously aromatic curry stock and you've got immediate access to a wonderful punch of flavour that makes it quick and easy to get an authentic, flavour-filled curry on the table in a flash. This makes a large batch, but it freezes brilliantly, and we use it as the base for the madras, vindaloo and balti recipes in this book (see pages 134–139), and it would also work brilliantly in the jalfrezi and tikka masala recipes in *BISH BASH BOSH!*, so the trickiest thing is choosing which to pick! .

Makes 4 litres

3 garlic cloves
3cm piece fresh ginger
1 tbsp vegetable oil
1 x 400g tin chopped
    tomatoes
4 litres water
6 large onions
4 medium carrots
3 tomatoes
1 green pepper
1 red pepper

For the spice mix
2 large bay leaves
1 tbsp curry powder
1 tbsp garam masala
1 tbsp ground turmeric
1 tbsp salt
1 tsp chilli powder
1 tsp coriander seeds
1 tsp ground coriander
1 tsp ground cumin
1 tsp peppercorns

5–6 litre stock pot or a large saucepan (to cook in batches) over a medium-high heat · Clean, sterilised freezer-safe containers

Start your stock · Peel and grate the garlic and ginger · Add the oil and all the spices to the pot along with the grated garlic and ginger · Cook for about 5 minutes · Add the chopped tomatoes · Pour in 500ml of the water and leave to simmer

Prep your veg · Peel and roughly chop the onions · Trim and roughly chop the other vegetables · Add all the veg to the pan along with 3½ litres of water · Lower the heat, cover the pot and simmer for about 1 hour, stirring occasionally

Finish your stock · Find and remove the bay leaves · Use a stick blender to blend the stock in the pan until completely smooth · Use straightaway or leave to cool to room temperature

Store · Divide the cool stock between containers and store for up to 3 months in the freezer

THAI GREEN & RED CURRY PASTES

Making your own curry paste is a brilliant way of elevating your curries from 'meh' to 'marvellous'. These pastes keep brilliantly in the freezer and defrost really quickly, so are great for making a big batch ahead and grabbing out of the freezer to make a speedy mid-week meal that feels really special. A top tip here is to freeze the curry pastes in ice-cube trays, then you can just defrost as many cubes as you need to make your curry and pop the rest back in the freezer, ensuring that nothing gets wasted. These pastes form the basis of the Thai curries in this book (see pages 186–189), but you can also use them to build your own delicious recipes.

THAI GREEN CURRY PASTE

Makes about 400g

4–6 fresh green chillies
16 garlic cloves
1 large onion
50g fresh ginger
2 limes
16 kaffir lime leaves
4 tsp black peppercorns
4 tsp ground coriander
4 tsp ground cumin
2 tsp salt
20g fresh coriander

Food processor or power blender

Make the paste • Stem the chillies • Peel the garlic cloves and ginger, then peel and roughly chop the onion • Zest the limes into a bowl and squeeze the juice over the top • Put the kaffir lime leaves, peppercorns, ground coriander, cumin and salt into the food processor or power blender and pulse into a powder • Add the rest of the ingredients and blitz to a paste

THAI RED CURRY PASTE

Makes about 400g

4–6 fresh red chillies
16 garlic cloves
1 large onion
20g fresh ginger
2 limes
4 tsp black peppercorns
4 tsp ground cumin
4 tsp ground coriander
2 tsp salt
16 kaffir lime leaves
10g fresh coriander

Food processor or power blender

Make the paste • Stem the chillies • Peel the garlic cloves and ginger, then peel and roughly chop the onion • Zest the limes into a bowl and squeeze the juice over the top • Put the peppercorns, ground cumin, ground coriander, salt and lime leaves in the food processor or power blender and blitz to a powder • Add the rest of the ingredients and blitz to a paste

LOCKDOWN LOAF

Lockdown made bakers of us all. Whether you were knocking up banana bread, rolling out cookies or stirring up sourdough, it seemed that we were all mastering a few new skills in the kitchen. Now the world has opened up again, many of us no longer have the time to feed and ferment our hungry dough babies on a daily basis, so something a bit simpler is in order. Enter the lockdown loaf, a chance to flex those baker's muscles and make a delicious home-baked loaf without having to book in a couple of days off work.

Makes 1 loaf

310g strong white
  bread flour
60g wholemeal or granary
  bread flour
10g salt
1 x 7g sachet fast-action
  dried yeast
260ml warm water
olive oil, for greasing

To serve
olive oil or dairy-free
  butter

Clean work surface dusted liberally with flour • Line a baking sheet with parchment paper • Dampen a clean tea towel • Small roasting tray

Make the dough • Measure the dry ingredients into a bowl • Pour in the water and mix to a dough • When the mixture comes together, use your hands to draw it all together into a sticky dough • Tip the dough on to the floured work surface and knead very firmly for 10 minutes, until smooth and elastic • Rinse out and lightly grease the mixing bowl with a little olive oil • Return the dough to the bowl and leave in a warm place for 1 hour

Knead • Gently knock the dough with your hand, pressing it down and deflating it a little • Tip it back on to the floured work surface, keeping its round shape • Pull the top semi-circle out a little then stick it down into the middle of the ball in a folding motion, then repeat with the bottom semi-circle and each side (we do this to create tension along the surface of the dough) • Flip it over and use your hands to cup and turn it to create a tight ball • Transfer to the lined baking sheet, drape in a damp tea towel and leave to rise for 30 minutes • Preheat the oven to 220°C

Bake the bread • Pour 50ml water into the roasting tray and put it on the bottom of the oven to create a little steam • Use a razor blade or a sharp scissors to snip into the top of the bread • Transfer the tray to the oven and bake for 18–20 minutes • Remove and transfer to a cooling rack to cool a little before eating warm, dipped in olive oil or spread with salted dairy-free butter

FOOLPROOF FOCACCIA

At BOSH!, our neighbours are always well fed, and this is Henry and Em-J's neighbour Carolyn's absolute favourite recipe. It's a big slab of brilliantly bubbly focaccia that feels celebratory placed in the middle of a table or served al fresco at a picnic or barbecue. The recipe couldn't be simpler, but for a little extra pizzazz, have a go at making your own art by arranging a glorious array of herbs and veg on top before baking. You could do a beautiful landscape, a vase of flowers or even portraits of your favourite vegan chefs . . . Tag us in your Instagram pics so we can see how you get on!

Serves 12

1 x 7g sachet fast-action
    dried yeast
2 tsp sugar
100ml + 1½ tbsp olive oil
340ml warm water
500g strong white
    bread flour
1 tsp fine salt
flaky sea salt
toppings of your choice,
    such as olives, capers,
    sundried tomatoes,
    finely sliced onion or
    rosemary leaves

To serve
olive oil
balsamic vinegar

Large mixing bowl • Clean work surface dusted liberally with flour • Cling film • 20 x 30cm baking tray • Parchment paper

Make the dough • Measure the yeast, sugar, the 1½ tablespoons olive oil and warm water into a jug • Measure the flour and salt into a large bowl and stir to mix • Make a well in the centre and pour in the yeast mixture • Use your hands to mix the liquid into the flour until it comes together as a sticky dough • Tip the dough on to the floured work surface • Work the dough for 10 minutes to activate the gluten, punching, turning and folding it, and resisting the urge to add more flour as wet dough will rise much better • When the dough starts to firm up and become springy, shape it into a really smooth ball • Clean out and grease the bowl then place the dough inside and cover with cling film • Set aside in a warm place for 1 hour to rise

Shape the dough • Pour 50ml of the olive oil into the baking tray and spread it around • Lay a sheet of parchment paper over the top and brush it with a little more oil • Tip the dough into the tray and coat it with the oil • Fold over the dough, turn it 45 degrees and fold again • Repeat a few times to create extra strength and layers • Stretch the dough out to cover most of the tin • Cover with cling film and set aside for another hour to rise

Bake your bread • Preheat the oven to 220°C • Uncover the focaccia and use your fingertips to press dimples into the dough • Drizzle with the remaining olive oil and then use your topping ingredients to decorate the top • Finish with a big pinch of flaky sea salt and then put the tray in the hot oven • Bake for 20 minutes, until golden on top • Allow to cool for a few minutes before sliding on to a cooling rack • Coat the top with a splash more olive oil while it's still hot • Slice and serve with oil, salt and balsamic vinegar

NUTRITION

When we first went vegan six-and-a-half years ago, our friends and families became quite concerned about nutrition. We were asked time and time again where we were planning to get our protein from and how we were going to get enough vitamins and nutrients on plant-based diets. The concern our nearest and dearest showed us was much appreciated and it inspired us to learn about vegan nutrition.

We learned, to our relief, that you can easily satisfy all your nutritional needs on a vegan diet. In fact, when approached properly, a vegan diet can be one of the healthiest diets there is! You can get all the nutrients, all the vitamins and all the protein you need to lead a healthy and abundant life.

We're pretty sure you've heard the expression 'you are what you eat' many times before, and even though we're not qualified nutritionists we think there's some truth in it. It stands to reason that if you eat healthily most of the time there's a high chance you'll be reasonably healthy, and if you eat unhealthily most of the time you probably won't be.

Healthy eating doesn't have to be difficult. In fact, it can be really easy, not to mention extremely delicious. All it takes is a bit of forward planning and a little discipline. In our book *Healthy Vegan* we came up with 5 golden rules to help make eating healthily on a vegan diet a little easier. Adopt these five straightforward rules and you'll be well on your way to becoming a healthier you!

1. The rainbow ratio: 50/25/25
Aim to eat about 50% fruits and veggies, 25% wholegrains and 25% protein. When people talk about 'a balanced diet', this is the ideal ratio: stick to it when you can.

2. Mix up your plate
Try to eat a broad and varied range of foods and colours at every meal. A mixture of colours, textures, spices and ingredients will provide your body with a broad range of health-promoting properties.

3. Eat your greens!
Your mum probably told you to eat your greens and mums usually know best, so get as much green in your diet as you can! Spinach, cavolo nero and kale are all great for green.

4. Aim for 80/20
80% healthy and 20% naughty. It's OK to eat naughty food from time to time; just remember to balance it out with healthy and colourful foods day to day.

5. Get your vitamins
We both use multivitamins on a daily (or nearly daily) basis. It's a simple, healthy habit to adopt that will make sure you're getting what you need, every day.

NUTRIENTS YOU NEED TO KNOW

Everyone, regardless of their dietary preferences, can have nutritional deficiencies, so everyone, vegans and non-vegans alike, should take their nutrition seriously.

Here's a handy list of nutrients, what they do and three great sources.

Vitamin A
Improves vision in dim light and helps your body's immune system
Butternut squash • carrots • spinach

Vitamin B12
Helps lift your mood, improves your energy levels and maintains your nerve cells
Nutritional yeast • yeast extract (like Marmite) • B12 supplements

Vitamin D
Great for mental health, helps prevent cancer and keeps your bones healthy
Mushrooms • fortified cereals • sunshine

Calcium
Aids brain function and strengthens your bones and teeth
Kale • tofu • almonds

Iron
Essential for healthy blood flow and good metabolism
Lentils • sweet potatoes • artichokes

Magnesium
Helps to repair and regenerate cells and provides you with energy
Spinach • black beans • bananas

Zinc
Aids and improves your immune system
Nuts • leafy green vegetables • oats

Fibre
Helps you manage your weight and promotes healthy gut bacteria
Berries, popcorn, whole grain pasta

Iodine
Helps your thyroid gland to function properly and important for normal growth of your body
Fortified almond milk • seaweed • iodine supplements

Omega 3
Helps maintain a healthy cardiovascular system and important for brain function
Walnuts • chia seeds • rapeseed oil

WHERE TO GET YOUR PROTEIN

One question someone on a vegan diet can expect to be asked at least once is 'where do you get your protein from?'

Here's a list of plant-based protein sources that that will help you answer that question.

Legumes
Such as beans, peas and lentils

Grains
Such as brown rice, quinoa and bulgur wheat

Nuts
Such as almonds, brazils and peanuts

Seeds
Such as chia, sunflower and pumpkin

Vegetables
Such as broccoli, kale and potatoes

Spreads
Such as hummus, tahini and nut butter

Other
Spirulina, dark chocolate and vegan protein powder

USEFUL CONVERSIONS

The recipes in this book use metric measurements, but if you want to scale a recipe up or down or are cooking somewhere in the world where you're more used to using a different unit of measurement (cups, for example), you can use the information on these two pages to make the required adjustments.

Oven temperatures

Temperatures can vary between ovens, so it is worth checking that yours is running at the correct heat by placing an oven thermometer inside. You may need to adjust the temperature if you know your oven runs particularly hot or cold. We cook in an electric fan oven, so if you use gas you may want to increase the oven temp slightly.

140°C	275°F	gas mark 1
150°C	300°F	gas mark 2
160°C	325°F	gas mark 3
180°C	350°F	gas mark 4
190°C	375°F	gas mark 5
200°C	400°F	gas mark 6
220°C	425°F	gas mark 7
230°C	450°F	gas mark 8
240°C	475°F	gas mark 9

Weight conversions

All of our recipes use metric (gram) measurements for dry ingredients. If you prefer to imperial (ounce) measurements then use the chart below to make the conversion. Most electronic cook's scales will switch between both, so use whichever you are happiest with.

25/30 g	1 oz
40 g	1½ oz
50 g	1¾ oz
55 g	2 oz
70 g	2½ oz
85 g	3 oz
100 g	3½ oz
115 g	4 oz
150 g	5½ oz
200 g	7 oz
225 g	8 oz
250 g	9 oz
300 g	10½ oz
350 g	12 oz
375 g	13 oz
400 g	14 oz
450 g	1 lb
500 g	1 lb 2 oz
600 g	1 lb 5 oz
750 g	1 lb 10 oz
900 g	2 lb
1 kg	2 lb 4 oz
2 kg	4 lb 8 oz

Volume conversions

We generally use metric measurements (ml/litres) for liquid ingredients such as water, stock, oil and dairy-free milk, though smaller amounts are measured in teaspoons or tablespoons. If you prefer to use imperial measurements (fl oz/pint) or cups, use the chart below work out the required amount.

5 ml	–	1 tsp
15 ml	½ fl oz	1 tbsp
30 ml	1 fl oz	2 tbsp
60 ml	2 fl oz	¼ cup
75 ml	2½ fl oz	⅓ cup
120 ml	4 fl oz	½ cup
150 ml	5 fl oz	⅔ cup
175 ml	6 fl oz	¾ cup
250 ml	8 fl oz	1 cup
350 ml	12 fl oz	1½ cups
500 ml	18 fl oz	2 cups
1 litre	1¾ pints	4 cups

Length

We use centimetres to measure short lengths. If you prefer to use inches, use the chart below to make the conversion.

1 cm	½ inch
2.5 cm	1 inch
3 cm	1¼ inches
5 cm	2 inches
8 cm	3¼ inches
10 cm	4 inches
20 cm	8 inches
25 cm	10 inches

Cup measures for dry ingredients

For dry ingredients, which are usually measured by weight, it is much harder to convert to a cup measurement as there is no universal rule; a cup of dairy-free butter weighs much more than a cup of flour, for example. The list below gives an approximate cup equivalent to the some of the ingredients that you may want to weigh in this way.

Flour	125 g	1 cup
Sugar (white)	200 g	1 cup
Sugar (brown)	200 g	1 cup
Sugar (icing)	130 g	1 cup
Dairy-free butter	225 g	1 cup (2 sticks)
Breadcrumbs (dried)	125 g	1 cup
Nuts	125 g	1 cup
Seeds	160 g	1 cup
Dried fruit	150 g	1 cup
Egg-free pasta (dried penne)	90 g	1 cup
Dried pulses (large)	175 g	1 cup
Grains & small pulses	200 g	1 cup

BIG THANKS!

Our creative team, who jumped through lots of lockdown-shaped hoops to get this awesome book over the line • Lizzie Mayson and Ollie Grove for the simply magnificent food photography • Nicky Johnston and Matthew Tortolano for the stunning pictures of us and our buddies • Rosie Ramsden, Sarah Vassallo, Georgia Rudd and Jemima Davis for styling the recipes so beautifully • Sarah Birks for making prop styling look so effortless • Em-J Williams for the awesome make-up and incredible banter • Alexis Knox for making sure our clothes were on point • Louis & Lucy from Larry King for the razor sharp haircuts

Our food team, who make absolutely sure our recipes are totally top notch and test them stringently to make sure they work perfectly, every single time: Elena Silcock, Rosie French, Katy McClelland, Christina Mackenzie and Sonali Shah, you really are ridiculously talented • Special thanks to our brother and phenomenally talented chef, Luke Robinson – as always, thanks for your culinary assistance and good times too!

Our publishing team, for turning the idea for this cookbook into a reality • Dan Hurst, you're supremely talented – we would have struggled to do this without you • Zoe Berville, this was our first project together, hopefully it will be the first of many! • Lisa Milton, another fantastic book under our belts, it's a joy working with you • Charlie Redmayne for being so committed to our cause • Lucy Sykes-Thompson at Studio Polka for the wonderful book design • Stephanie Heathcote for the all-round A* design work • Caroline McArthur for your fantastic copy-editing skills • Halema Begum, Charlies Light and Sarah Davis for the marvellous production • Georgina Green, Fliss Porter, Harriet Williams, Darren Shoffren, Angela Thomson, Marta Juncosa, Jay Cochrane, Debbie McNally, Kelly Webster and Laura Daley for being a truly world class sales team • Joanna Rose, Dawn Burnett, Noleen Robinson, Jen Callahan-Packer, Sophie Calder and Ben Hurd for doing such a good job at getting our books such great exposure • Helen Povey for allowing us to use your lushy studio • Abigail Le Marquand-Brown for being such an assistant extraordinaire

TEAM BOSH! Thank you for dedicating your working lives to such a worthy cause. You're getting a lot of plants on a lot of plates, and that's important • Nat, you're a hero – we're lucky to have you • Cat, you've been with us since (almost) day dot, we appreciate you more than you know • Bev, we've done some great things together, we can't wait to do more! • Tom, Aoife and everyone at Bev James, you're legends • Megan and everyone at Carver PR, the work we've done together has put vegan food in front of tens of millions of people – don't underestimate how powerful that is • Guy Mottershead for helping us build a brand that is literally good enough to eat • Gail for professionalising our branding and Curly for tightening up our copy so well • Charlie Harris, aka The Chizzler, we had a blast. Best of luck with your next chapter bro

Henry's people • EmJ & Chippy • Jane & Mark • Alice & Graham • Chris, Paul & Tom Williams • Sukey, Nick, Gus & Arthur • Bruce, thinking of you x • Claire, Nick & Xander • Alison & Curtis • John Dodd, Zoe & Stanley • Davey P, Ben & Rosie

Ian's people • Sarah • Mum, Dad, Frances, Stew & Phoebe • Carolyn, Edward & Philip • Robin & Suzie • Simon • Josephine, Katie, Mike & Kev • Steve, Shirley, Lynsey & Kerry • Paul, Sue, Nick, Lesley & Alexander, Sean, Alex & Meg, Jamie & Milly, Mikey & Elektra

Our good buds • Alex, Tara & Cillian • Darren & Danielle • Anna & Beth • Mutty • Nat, Khairan, Lennox and Ziyah • Marcus, Ellie, Jasper, Caspian & Nia • Ekow, Claire, Hugo & Xander • Zulf, Farhana, Ayza, Ayla & Rumi • Alex Farbz, Cat, Freddie & Samuel • Addison, Claire, Lola Grace & Stanley • Kweku, Angie & Akaiya • Tom, Emilie, Alex & Ruby • Martha, Duncan & Ernie • Josh, Charlotte, Leo, Uma & Bump • Tim, Susie, Wren & Ember • Akash & Dilshad • Nick, Ruth & Finn • Maso, Bex, Finn & Bump • Tom, Stef & Romy • CB & Nikita • Luke & Kasia • Nish & Rachel • Janey & Jack • Joe, Ted and the fam • Jenny • Louis • Leslie • Ayo • All Prosecco Club

Everyone we know working in and around the vegan food space • You know who you are and we salute you • Everyone we don't know working in the vegan food space, we salute you too

Super special thank you to everyone who follows us on social media. Every like, share and comment ensures our vegan food videos are seen by millions

Most importantly, you • You're holding a cookbook that's full of plant-based food; if more decided to introduce more plant-based food into their diets, just like you have, the world would be in much better shape

INDEX